Bewitch a Man

Bewitch a Man

HOW TO FIND HIM AND KEEP HIM UNDER YOUR SPELL

FIONA HORNE

SIMON SPOTLIGHT ENTERTAINMENT
New York   London   Toronto   Sydney

SIMON SPOTLIGHT ENTERTAINMENT

An imprint of Simon & Schuster

1230 Avenue of the Americas, New York, New York 10020

Text copyright © 2006 by Fiona Horne

SIMON SPOTLIGHT ENTERTAINMENT and related logo are trademarks of Simon & Schuster, Inc.

Designed by Steve Kennedy

Manufactured in the United States of America

10 9 8 7 6 5 4 3

Library of Congress Cataloging in Publication Data

Horne, Fiona, 1966-

Bewitch a man : how to find him and keep him under your spell / Fiona Horne.

p. cm.

ISBN-13: 978-1-4169-1474-7

ISBN-10: 1-4169-1474-9

1. Love—Miscellanea. 2. Man-woman relationships—Miscellanea. 3. Witchcraft—Miscellanea. 4. Magic—Miscellanea. I. Title.

BF1572.L6H67 2006

646.7'7—dc22

2006023076

$\mathcal{A}$CKNOWLEDGMENTS

Much love and brightest blessings to all the wonderful people at Simon Spotlight Entertainment, especially Jen B. and Patrick for your support and gorgeous friendship.

And thank you to YOU for reading this book. I hope it puts a smile on your face and in your heart! Please visit me at my website: www.fionahorne.com!

TABLE OF CONTENTS

Introduction

YHI IS MY FAVORITE GODDESS FROM AUSTRALIAN Aboriginal mythology. She is the goddess of light and creation, a sun deity who lived in the dream time. When she opened her eyes, light fell on Earth. She then walked the earth, and green things grew where her steps fell. Soon the whole world was covered with plants, fruits, trees, and flowers. She next decided that, in addition to plants, she wanted to make something that could dance and move. Insects of all kinds were created. Then she explored ice caves in a mountain. She shone her light inside and fish and lizards came out, along with countless kinds of birds, mammals, and amphibians. But ultimately Yhi returned to her own world, and when she left, darkness came back and covered Earth. But the next day Yhi opened her eyes again from her home in the sky, and her light returned for all to enjoy.

Many millennia later, Yhi saw something strange. It was a man, alone, and she realized he was not anything she had created, and she was intrigued. While the man slept that night, Yhi focused all her power on a flower so that it became more magnificent than anything any god had ever created. When Man awoke, he, joined by all the other animals of Yhi's creation, gazed in awe at the beautiful flower. The flower then blossomed and turned into Woman. She looked at Man and found him interesting. Man ran around doing many things to try to impress her and wanted nothing more than to make Woman happy. She was amused and thrilled—in fact, all creation was laughing and enjoying their coupling, declaring man and woman good for each other.

So, a female deity created our world and Woman from her own light and the beauty of a flower. She created everything *except* Man (who knows *where* he came from?!). But Man's job was to impress and amuse Woman.

Sounds like an ideal world. So what the heck happened? It turns out man forgot his role in the whole scheme of things. Well, it is up to us to remind him, to take back the power.

Bewitchers-to-be, what are we waiting for? Let's go bewitch a man (or two or three).

Chapter One

WHY BEWITCHING?

AFTER WRITING A NUMBER OF BOOKS ON WITCHCRAFT AND trying to always be "politically correct"—sidestepping difficult subjects such as conjuring love in a particular person or giving out information that was potentially too powerful—I decided to write *Bewitch a Man*. Like you, I've experienced long periods of feeling unhappy and unloved by a decent man. For some, a long time is a few months, for others, it could be years. And it's so frustrating. You've done all the right things to lift yourself out of the relationship rut: self-improvement courses, positive meditation at your twice-weekly yoga class, the "How to Meet the Millionaire of Your Dreams" Learning Annex workshop. You close your eyes and spin your little heart out on the bike at the gym five times a week so that you have buns of sexy steel (or as close as you are ever going to get). You've read *He's Just Not That Into You* over and over and dutifully swallowed its bitter dating-reality pill. You're even a member of three Internet dating services and two book clubs and a salsa dance class . . . and yet, you are *still* single.

Is spell casting to get a man any crazier than some of the other things we do?

I remember, when I was younger and less wise, being totally in love with a local punk-rock star who liked to hang out at the neighborhood pub on Saturdays and play pinball. To catch his eye, I would travel to the pub during my lunch hour to practice like mad playing that pinball machine. He was so blown away when I outscored him after three months of lunchtime practicing. Of course, I got fired from my job for being late back to work so many times. Yet, did he ask me out? Not until a year later when my all-girl punk band toured with his band. Then we were girlfriend-boyfriend for two years until he left me for his sister's best friend. I still wonder what she had for a high score.

Bewitchery is empowering. We shouldn't downgrade our personal choices or minimize our goddess-given talents to impress a guy. Hey, if we do, he isn't worth impressing in the first place. Doing something cool that celebrates and expresses your uniqueness is going to get the attention of a man—and not just any man but the *right* man. The beauty and brilliance of spell casting is that it is anchored in ancient, potent practices that resonate in the deepest parts of our DNA—in our collective unconsciousness, in the pulse of our blood.

With my assured guidance, it's not hard to understand magick and experience its positive effects. Face it, life is magickal. The process of creation that our own bodies are capable of is extraordinary. Just because we numb and dumb ourselves down to deal with the pressure of modern society and the pressures of competing, excelling, or just simply surviving in a really difficult situation doesn't mean that the magick isn't out there. It really is. And bewitchery is universally spiritual; anyone can do it—Christian, Jew (or Jewitch like me!), and Muslim. And lose your preconceptions: Bewitchery is not about summoning demons. It's about working with energy, light, love, and your own will! In fact, this whole book is a spell that can enchant your love life.

Bewitch a Man

So what do you have to lose? Suspend your disbelief, cynicism, and fear, and let yourself experience something extraordinary. Remember, every woman was put on this earth to be happy and in love—at least once! Spell casting is not crazy or weird—just a really great help. It works very practically and positively. It's sexy and creative.

The only way to go from here is up—and trust me, you will! Watch out, world. There are going to be a lot of women now enjoying love with great guys and in numbers that could tip the scales back to a matriarchal world. Remember, the major way women are disempowered in a patriarchal society is by being unhappy in love. It's time to reclaim what's yours.

Be prepared to allow something extraordinary to happen in your life. Magick isn't mumbo jumbo and superstitious nonsense. Think about it. If a woman stands under a full moon and lights incense, calls on the gods, and confers spiritual power that can transform reality, it is called witchcraft, and it is considered bad. If a man does all this under the roof of a church, he is called a priest and considered holy and in direct and superior communion with God.

But here is an important point to make as you start

on the path of a Bewitcher—you must not brag about your bewitchery. You will learn something cool that expresses your uniqueness, but I offer that solely for your (and fellow Bewitchers') enjoyment and appreciation. Just let the man accept you and adore you for your total package. Keep your tricks up your sleeve!

You don't have to do everything offered in this book at once—too much information can overload and shock you into apathy and inaction. Just be aware: It is not how much you know. It's what you do with what you *do* know.

SO, HOW DO SPELLS WORK?

Look to science for an answer on how spells work. In the world of quantum physics there are subatomic particles whose energy can be measured only when they are being observed. That is, they are invisible unless our consciousness is actively engaged in their reality. *The observed becomes changed by the observer.* So it is with spell casting: We allow ourselves to "know" the reality of what we are creating, and in doing so, it exists. And sometimes the result will be better than you can possibly imagine. You must keep an open mind when spell

Bewitch a Man

casting (like with anything in life) and focus more on the journey than on the destination.

There is a wonderful card in the tarot deck called the Fool. The Fool is represented by zero—meaning all things and nothing. He is pictured leaping off a cliff, head flung back, arms outstretched, with a flower in his mouth. One night when I was meditating on this card, I imagined him calling out, *Catch me, universe! I am looking forward to seeing where I land*. This has become my mantra every time I take a leap into the unknown and attempt to conjure something new and exciting into my life. It is precisely this joyful abandon and trust in the knowledge that you are a child of the universe and ultimately deserving of love and happiness that will be your most powerful ally in spell casting. Know that something will happen, not always in the way you expect. I have experienced over and over again that what you get is usually better than what you thought you needed.

So now that I have got you excited, you need to absorb these five easy steps of spell casting success into the matrix of your consciousness (basically, this means just read them and don't zone out as you do).

STEP ONE

it's easier than you think

Is a short easy spell weaker than a long hard spell? No! When you are making magick, time doesn't mean anything. Ten seconds of being completely focused in the moment is more powerful than ten hours of trying to focus on a candle flame, dying of boredom. You know how your most intense dreams seem to go on forever? Well, in reality our most intense dreams actually last no more than thirty seconds. It's the same concept here. A few seconds of bewitchery can have more effect on your life than a few hours of struggling to concentrate. You just have to make the commitment to really focus, and then . . .

STEP TWO

you have to know only one thing

Believe in yourself and your ability to do something extraordinary—and then concentrate and apply your efforts from that place of personal power.

Bewitch a Man

STEP THREE
have fun

Excitement and optimism are the two most essential ingredients for successful spell casting. Your positive passion is the fuel for the magickal fire that cooks your spell.

STEP FOUR
get messy

Get really involved and into what you are doing. Don't overthink or be hesitant. Instead, be confident and let your enthusiasm for what you are doing explode as you whip up a potion or conjure up a charm. Intuition will guide you, and if you feel like changing the spell on the spur of the moment—do it. Your gut is always right when you are acting from a place of positive self-belief and self-respect.

STEP FIVE
walk away and don't look back

Doing a spell is like planting a seed: You don't keep digging it up to see how it's growing. Do your spell and walk away, and don't keep going over it in your head. Leave it alone and let the magick do its work.

When people ask me if I cast spells and I say yes, their immediate comment is, "Well, don't cast one on me." And I reply, "Why not? It may be a nice spell!"

Because of the all-pervading negativity in Western society, most people assume that spells are bad before they contemplate that they could be for good. The most important aspect of spell casting is that a Bewitcher needs to understand that what she sends out comes back—more often than not, magnified a few times over. Thus, it is always more beneficial to concentrate on the good of your newfound power. You want your presence in the world to attract amazing, fortuitous energy and not darkness and difficulty.

Remember, magick is fueled by your intent—so the more passionate and intense you get about what you're doing, the better. Darker emotions like anger and lust are very potent emotions—great for channeling into spell casting, where that raw energy can be transformed into a giant fuel cell to kick magickal butt. But the downfall of spell casting when you are extremely angry or in a heightened state of lust is that your energy cannot be focused in a pure positive stream to really get the results that you need.

Bewitch a Man

The book you hold in your hands is racy and life changing, challenging and shocking. But I know just from your picking it up that you are ready for some serious excitement in your life and, more important, positive change in your love life.

> *"Fiona Horne is truly an amazing witch, and I have seen her practical magick firsthand. Recently, I had a problem with my boyfriend, who was being inattentive and noncommittal. I consulted with Fiona, who did a little ritual with me and gave me some advice, which I immediately took. Within a few weeks my boyfriend was back in my arms and has been more than attentive and truly committed to me!"*
> —DEVIN DEVASQUEZ,
> ACTRESS AND PLAYBOY COVER GIRL

> *"Just by reading Fiona's love spells, I have found that magickal things happen!"*
> —DANNII MINOGUE, SINGER AND ACTRESS

Chapter Two

Getting Started— A Bewitcher's Bible

SOME OF THE THINGS YOU ARE ABOUT TO READ MAY seem unbelievable, even at times silly and pointless. If you think they are unbelievable, silly, and pointless, then indeed they will be. I am not going to try to convince you otherwise. But you bought this book to bewitch a man. The first lesson is that you must *believe* something extraordinary is about to happen in your life—and that often the sillier and more pointless something appears, the more powerful its effect on your life will be.

There are a lot of relationship books out there filled with terrific practical advice. But they are lacking reliable magickal advice. Combine the two approaches and you can't fail. *Bewitching works . . . with all the passion, excitement, and intent with which you fuel it.* Approach it with trepidation, cynicism, and doubt, and you won't bewitch a man. You'll bore him.

CHECKLIST FOR SUCCESSFUL BEWITCHERY

✓ Believe in your bewitching power.
✓ Practice your bewitchments.
✓ Study the rules of bewitchery.
✓ Memorize the mantras of bewitchery.

BE REALISTIC WHEN BEWITCHING YOUR MAN

By this I mean the sky is the limit, but it's not outer space. Please don't try to bewitch Brad Pitt; our honorary Bewitcher leader, Angelina Jolie, has already done that! There is a reason that a lot of spell casting books emphasize that you should not try to interfere with another's free will and "make" someone fall in love with you. It is because manipulated and make-believe love so often backfire against the Bewitcher. When you cast your bewitchments, it is recommended that you don't specify a particular person—just describe the *attributes* of the person that you desire. Then let the universe decide which guy is best for you; he will most likely exceed what you asked for. If you insist on aiming your bewitchment at a particular person, just brace yourself for a wild, unpredictable ride!

BEWITCHERS' RULES

1. **Bewitchers always put themselves first—bewitching a man is easy.**

   Bewitching yourself is much harder, and you actually can't bewitch a man until you can work your magick on yourself. Instead of working so hard to please him, work harder to please yourself . . . because ultimately this is what will please him.

2. Thou shalt love thyself—no matter what.

If you don't love yourself, who will? Only another person as miserable as you. If you want to hate or even slightly dislike yourself and be miserable, why are you reading this book? Get your act together and be ready to rise up like the warrioress you are—powerful, potent, positive, and completely bewitching.

3. Bewitchers never discuss their relationships or love magick with mortal girls (and hardly ever with fellow Bewitchers).

Think of a balloon that is being blown up. If you keep opening the neck to peer inside, it is going to deflate. It is exactly the same principle when you are casting spells and conducting bewitchery. There is a witches' spell-casting rule: When you cast a spell, walk away without looking back; do not discuss it with anyone else under any circumstances until the spell has worked.

4. Bewitchers define themselves and their lives and are very independent.

When most mortal girls are obsessing over whether to call a date or their boyfriend, and acting needy and codependent when they are with him, Bewitchers are relishing their alone time to continue concocting their spells and magick to keep him bewitched, as well as doing things for themselves that make them feel good.

It is a tremendous privilege to be alive in this extraordinary world. By the positive, empowered choices you make, the beauty and brilliance of this world will be mirrored and magnified for all, but most important, for you.

5. Bewitchers do not have a "use by" date.

Bewitchers don't get older; we get better.

6. Bewitchers are disciplined in their methods.

Sometimes to get to the bottom of a problem that is preventing personal happiness, it takes a lot of writing, chanting, and waving incense sticks around! A Bewitcher does not shy away from the responsibilities of her magick.

7. Bewitchers like to look good and do so at every opportunity.

Bewitching is not a fashion statement—it's more of a spiritual statement—but that doesn't mean you can't be fashionable. And thank the Goddess that black is the new black—everyone can wear it again! One can look so archetypically bewitchy *and* so chic.

And as I like to say, "Cleanliness is next to goddessliness!" By cleaning your body, you are also cleaning your mind. So scrub yourself in the shower or bath, and as that water swirls down the drain, see it taking all negativity with it. Then pamper yourself with potions and creams, get your hair done, and revel in your bewitching beauty.

8. **Bewitchers never get down on themselves or depressed when a budding bewitchery doesn't work out.**

    Let go gracefully when you suspect you have misfired your powers. Giving up an opportunity merely means an opportunity is created for something else.

9. **Bewitchers turn up their favorite music every day and dance like no one's watching—no matter what!**

    Music is the voice of the soul, and when you get up and pound your feet, wave your arms, throw your head back with a big smile, your heart rising in a thrilling rhythmic pulse, that is when the most ancient strands of your DNA awaken, and you are connected to all your ancestors and all your descendants, and plugged into the source of universal joy. And on a less esoteric level, as endorphins flood your body, your skin will glow, your eyes will glisten, and you will exude super-radiant, sexy bewitching power. Men everywhere will fall at your feet.

10. **Bewitchers share the love.**

    We are into making our sisters feel good. We choose to see ourselves not as surrounded by rivals in our attempts to bewitch a man, but friends and compatriots who mutually encourage our goals. So compliment your sisters, make them smile, motivate them, support them—share the love—and love will be shared with you.

THE HUNDREDTH MONKEY

In the early 1950s, scientists studied a type of monkey on a Japanese island. Some of these monkeys learned to wash sweet potatoes before eating them, and this behavior spread to other monkeys through the usual fashion of observation and mimicking. Nothing so amazing about that, you say? Well, what is amazing is that once a certain number of monkeys had learned the skill—the *hundredth* monkey—the learned behavior was absorbed into the collective consciousness of the same monkey species on surrounding islands, yet none of those monkeys had ever previously washed their sweet potatoes before eating them.

The theory has generated controversy and mainstream science generally discredits the phenomenon. But isn't that the way of the mainstream? To discredit something that potentially can give people an empowered sense of unity and community? I prefer to believe that an individual *can* contribute positively to the greater whole by one smile or one positive thought.

"Fiona is a priestess of positive power! She creates wonderful spells that empower, enlighten, and

Bewitch a Man

enhance our ability to experience positive love in life. Her unique magickal advice is very popular with my listeners. I enjoy having her on my show so much I could call myself a 'Bewitchling' now!"

—LEEZA GIBBONS, TELEVISION
PERSONALITY AND RADIO HOST

BEWITCHERS' MANTRAS

Memorize these and repeat them to yourself regularly. I know you are "chomping at the bit" to get to the spells—but these mantras are *very* important, for they prepare you with the proper receptive mind-set so that magick can *really* work in your life.

1. **Obstacles are not there to stop me but to guide me to a better opportunity.**
   Every wrong guy who makes you unhappy and turns your mind into a pretzel as you try to fathom his motives and behavior is guiding you toward the person that is *not* going to do this.

2. **The universal ruler of love is conspiring in my favor.**
   Bewitchers stay positive and strong always. Or they do a spell or ritual that sets their heads straight.

3. **I am a noble warrioress.**
   Every Bewitcher knows that the universe always

rewards the most bold and noble members with the hardest of trials because these people are capable of fighting—and winning—the hardest battles. The tougher and more disappointing life (read: your love life) gets, the more complimented you can feel. You would not be getting so much grief dumped on you if you weren't capable of throwing it off. Know that your blossoming bewitchery will increase the odds so that you *win!*

4. I am a star.

No, this doesn't mean that Bewitchers are obsessed with being celebrities. "I am a star" means Bewitchers understand that there is a simple potent power in the star shape. In ancient bewitchery, the image of a human being standing with legs and arms outstretched encased in a star was prevalent.

A Bewitcher is the star of her own life and embraces all the good stuff that fact brings with it. If you don't believe me, lie down right now and spread your arms and legs out in a star position—the wider your arms and legs, the bigger star that you are. Stay there for five minutes with your eyes closed and a big smile on your face. Sit up. Don't you feel fabulous? Do this exercise as often as possible. As you do it, you are turning yourself into a living talisman of the most positive, bewitching energy in the universe. You will be blessing yourself and all your efforts with good luck.

5. **Forgive them . . . they know not what they do.**
Yes, I borrowed this from Jesus but I know he won't mind. He loved everyone equally and wanted us girls to be just as happy as the guys. This mantra reminds us to stop trying to figure out guys (or trying to change them, which is a fruitless and draining activity) and just accept them as they are. If they are behaving really appallingly, should you be inflicting yourself with their company? Probably not.

Stars are seen as the ultimate symbol of blessing and empowerment. Four points represent the magick nature elements of air, earth, fire, and water, and the top fifth point represents "spirit," which is our divine consciousness. Surround yourself with stars wherever possible and reap the rewards of positive energy! Get good at drawing them on everything—from your notes on how you are getting a promotion at work, to the back of your business cards that you hand out to men you may decide to bewitch.

6. **RA!!**
Ra is the Egyptian name of the sun god. Said out

loud, it should sound like an animal growl! When you cry his name, you invoke an ancient energy that scares away any bad vibes surrounding you and lights up your inner being with pure light. Bewitchers need to shine strong and bright through all the murky twists and turns that love and being a girl in the modern world can bring. So say "RA!" whenever you need a shot of fire in your veins and spirit.

7. **I am a Bewitcher. I have power over men.**
   Say this as often as possible—too many times is not enough!

> *"Fiona's magickally practical advice has really helped me feel strong and empowered in my relationships. For many years I have struggled with finding 'Mr. Right' and felt there were only 'Mr. Wrongs' everywhere. My attitude has changed, and now the only problem I have is choosing which 'Mr. Right' I want."*
> —ANITA, PERSONAL ASSISTANT,
> WEST HOLLYWOOD

BEWITCHMENT BASH

n. a little party one throws oneself when deciding to embark on the path of bewitchery and bewitch a man
    Be aware that when you throw yourself this party,

you are committing yourself to being a Bewitcher, someone who is bold, magickal, and bewitching. And that's a great thing.

PREPARATION

You need to get a few things together to do the bewitchment. Nothing too crazy—I won't have you running around trying to find little black bats, cats' claws, and doves' blood! Just grab the few things I mention below and have a blast!

camera

Just like you would want photos taken of your wedding, you will want a photo of your bewitchment, to document a wonderful turning point in your life—the moment when you decided to embrace and enjoy without boundaries your personal power. If you start to weaken on your resolve to be a magickal, empowered creature, you can go back, look at the photos, relive the magick, and re-empower yourself.

libations

As a part of your bewitchment, you will be drinking your favorite champagne—sacred to Erzulie, the voodoo goddess of love and enchantment. If you are a nondrinker, pomegranate juice is a great alternative. The fruit is a particularly potent source of love energy.

sweet treats

Create a beautiful, lush organic fruit bowl, featuring sweet berries, juicy melons, and red apples. Cut the apples in half—side to side, not top to bottom. This is to expose the star-shaped arrangement of the seeds, which in the world of bewitchery represents great love and power. All these succulent fruits are representative of the great male bounty that you are now going to attract with your blossoming bewitching powers.

flowers

Decorate the space where you are having your bewitchment with lovely, luscious flowers. Flowers are spirit blossoms—they are nature's depiction of the great beauty that lies at the heart of all creation. The more fabulous the flower, the more love beauty you will be blessed with. Let your personal needs be your guide. I am partial to large, white, heavily scented lilies and rose petals, strewn everywhere. They represent sweet purity of intent and love manifesting in every aspect of life.

one white candle

Make it a thick, sweetly scented pillar candle—it will embody the powerful catalytic energy of fire, representative of the great positive changes about to take place in your love life.

Set up your bewitchment bash like you would a party you were holding for a very special guest. Arrange the flowers, scatter the petals, and set out the fruits and libations in a lovely bowl and glassware. Place the candle in a prominent position and put on some great chill music.

look beautiful

For your bash wear something lovely that you feel like a love goddess in. Or you can chose to be *sky clad*. "Clad by the sky"—that is, you are naked. Sky clad to Bewitchers is a pure and perfectly beautiful state *no matter what your size or shape*.

WHAT TO DO

Light the candle, and by its light slowly eat some of the fruit and drink. Know that in this sacred space empowered by your intent everything you are eating and drinking is enchanted. Think about what you have learned already from this book and how it is going to manifest powerfully in your life. See yourself happy and in love.

At this point it is appropriate to take a photo of yourself. If you feel like getting up and dancing slowly and sensuously, please do. Luxuriate in yourself and celebrate your existence.

When you are ready, gaze at the candle flame, and in its glow see reflected the infinite light and depth of your personal bewitching power. Feel your heart open ecstatically in your chest, unfolding like a flower, and emphatically state these words:

Alone and strong,
right here, right now
I am beautiful, passionate, and proud!
I awaken to bewitchery
for the good of all
but mostly for me.

Let these words resonate through your being and then pour some champagne on the ground as a libation to the great goddess. (If you are having your bewitchment in an apartment, pour some onto a plant.)

When you are partied out, snuff the candle (don't blow it out; you will blow away the magick!)

and go to bed. You will dream of how powerful and amazingly bewitching you are, knowing that tomorrow you will awake to a magickal world full of infinite potential, a new chapter of your life.

"Every time I have Fiona on the air, the phones GO CRAZY!! Based on the volume of calls and e-mails (and requests from my girlfriends), there is obviously a large number of people looking for a little guidance and help from 'out there' . . . whether they're recovering from a breakup, looking for 'the ONE,' or everything in between. Fiona is a breath of fresh air compared to those critical 'self-help know-it-alls' and adds a unique approach to the power of positive thinking. How do you know, if YOU DON'T TRY???!!!"
—LISA FOXX, ON-AIR PERSONALITY, STAR (98.7, LOS ANGELES & 101.3, SAN FRANCISCO)

Chapter Three

BASIC SPELLS, CHARMS, AND RITUALS FOR BEWITCHING

BEWITCHERS MUST THINK DIFFERENTLY FROM everyone else. They are not locked in a depressed, fatalistic attitude when it comes to the difficulties of finding love in this world. Simply by having a different attitude, you can shape your world to be more favorable and appealing. By looking at things differently, things actually become different. How can you change your miserable point of view? By being disciplined in your thoughts. It is sometimes really hard. But know that you have the power as a Bewitcher to make things better.

Change your thoughts, act differently, and your world will be different.

It is hard to think differently from everyone else, to see the cup as half-full, not half-empty. But it is a skill Bewitchers must master. Constant vigilance of our thoughts is mandatory. Anytime we pessimistically feel that there is no true love out there for us, we must close our eyes, shake our heads hard, and change the dialogue to: *I am single because I am so damn special; only a very special man is worthy of my company.*

So, you have read the rules, memorized your mantras, thrown yourself a bewitchment bash, and started to embrace the concept of the brand-new you. It is now time to begin flexing those magickal muscles, taking some basic spells out for a test drive. This chapter is devoted to getting Mr. Right to notice the wonderful Bewitcher right under his nose. Following are some of the most powerful love spells and bewitchery ever to appear in a modern book. If you have got this far, they can work for you. It's time to give love another chance and get ready for romance!

SHE'S GOT THE LOOK

"The look" is a terrific bewitching skill that requires a little practice but is very simple. It's a combination of practical and magickal skill. The practical side involves getting your pupils to dilate at will. This is something that naturally happens when we look at someone or something we deeply love, or when we have an orgasm. When our pupils dilate, we are immediately more attractive to the opposite sex.

Making your pupils dilate at will, without the endorphin rush of love, involves simply focusing on something small. For example, rather than looking at someone in the eyes, stare at an eyelash or the corner of one of his eyes. As you focus on that minute area, your pupils will naturally dilate to let in more light, causing your gaze to subconsciously appear to him as more mysterious and compelling.

As you perfect the practical part of this task, you must now incorporate the magickal. Using your imagination, picture a stream of soft red light flowing from your eyes that bathes your target in a seductive glow. You will weave him into your web of desire, and he will be putty in your hands. In your head repeat the words *You are mine, you are mine* for added effect.

"The look" appears simple, but it is actually quite a complex skill to effectively master so that you don't look like a cross-eyed weirdo, but look incredibly magnetic instead. Practice it by looking at yourself in

Bewitch a Man

the mirror. Then go out and practice it at nightclubs, in bars, on the bus, at the library, anywhere you like. You can incorporate "the look" into many of your bewitchments and magickal practices that involve interacting with the man you are bewitching.

THE "I AM PICKING HIM UP WITHOUT A DOUBT" RITUAL

This is a simple ritual that works to make you feel sexy. And again, the sex appeal you radiate is the first port of call for a man's attention, being the basic beasts that they are.

Light lots of candles and place them in the bathroom and in your bedroom. As you put match to wick, say these words:

I light a flame of passion

Know that you are working with the energy of fire—potent, passionate, and fast acting. When you fuel a simple action like lighting a candle with magickal intent, you are surrounding yourself with flames of passion, fueling your aura with magnetic male-attracting power.

Take a shower or bath and slowly massage yourself, awakening to the subtle sexy pleasures of touch. Close your eyes and imagine your bewitched man touching your skin, with his main purpose being only to please you. Really focus on seeing yourself as an irresistible creature worthy of great love and adoration. As you massage yourself, imagine his arms wrapped around you, your hands are his hands, and mutter these words over and over:

My will is great.
You will not escape.

You are weaving a spell of "pickup potential"—any man that you set your eyes on and decide you want will not be able to escape your charm and your intent. Get dressed slowly, clothing yourself as if you were wrapping the most valuable piece of delicate china in the universe. Make up your face and smile at yourself in the mirror the whole time.

Before you leave the house, "kiss out" the candles (blow a kiss at them as you blow them out), knowing you are blowing away anything negative in your path.

DEVIOUS WAY TO BEWITCH A MAN

The following bewitchery is actually more mischievous than devious; it requires you to be playful yet fearless, brave yet shameless, as you lure into your web the man of your desire without him even realizing what is happening until it's too late!

Sit behind the guy you see on the same train/bus everyday, whom you have a crush on. Check out his shoulders intently. If you see a stray fallen hair there, carefully take it (without anyone spotting you) and wrap it in some tissue that you keep in your pocket expressly for this purpose.

When you get home, set a pink or red candle in a jar and carefully place the hair inside the jar, keeping it from touching the wick. Light the candle and as the wax melts, let the hair get captured. Do *not* let the hair catch fire. If it does, the spell won't work and you will have to get another hair.

When the hair is floating in the wet wax, snuff the flame. Let the wax harden. Next, light the candle in the morning and at night. Before you put match to wick, breathe over the surface, saying these words:

Bound to my will you are.
You shall be close to my heart.

Let it burn for five minutes before snuffing the flame.

If you do this for seven days, you will definitely speak and connect with your stranger on the train/bus and at the very least get a date with him. What you do after that is dependent upon whether you like him or not. Remember: He is bewitched, so he will follow your lead.

THE "LET YOUR HAIR DOWN" RITUAL

Rapunzel, let down your hair! There's more than a fairy tale going on here.

Ancient bewitchery lore says that a witch's power is multiplied by letting down her hair during a spell. To try this, release your hair at the same time that you direct your magick, and it will really reach your target. If you have short hair, the same can be achieved with props. For instance, try gathering and releasing the hem of your skirt, or if you are at a restaurant, unfurl a rolled-up napkin. You can even undo your belt or have a shoulder strap slip down as a substitute. Or come prepared with a strand of your hair in your pocket, and release it to the wind when you do your magick.

Bewitch a Man

So, when you are in the presence of the man you desire, let down your "hair." No one will know what you are doing, other than being subtly seductive. And as you do so, visualize your magickal, bewitching energy flowing from your action. You will exude a magnetic attraction that no man can resist.

A SPELL TO DETERMINE SOMEONE'S AFFECTIONS

If you feel you are getting mixed signals from a guy and want to know whether he really cares for you, do this spell:

Buy a handkerchief and get his initials embroidered on it. If you are a wiz at embroidering, it's even more powerful if you can do it yourself.

Next, dab it with some of your signature perfume.

Go outside or to a window where you can see the moon clearly in the sky. Hold the hankie close to your heart, close your eyes, and visualize the person you desire.

Chant these words three times:

If you love me, let me know.

Then open your eyes, gaze at the moon, and say the following:

With this charm, his love now shows.

Keep the charmed hankie close to your heart—charmed by the moon and your intent, the hankie is now like a homing signal. Next time you see the person, notice any form of new behavior he exhibits. If he seems to talk with or look at you more often than usual, this is a sign that he feels love for you.

A word of caution: For the spell to truly succeed, it's recommended that you at least have a hunch that he has some kind of feelings for you in the first place. The spell is very subtle in its action and is usually ideal for situations where the Bewitchling and the bewitched have timid personalities. It gets you both over the first hurdle. Of course, once you are a full-fledged Bewitcher, timidity has no place in your repertoire!

A MEDIEVAL LOVE CHARM REBORN IN MODERN TIMES

In the days before toothpaste, breath fresheners, and mint candy, there was an old spell that everyday people could cast that involved studding a lemon with whole cloves and then offering it to a loved one. Rather than taking offense and thinking you were implying that their breath stank, it was actually seen as an invitation for a kiss! The loved one would take a clove from the lemon, place it on his or her tongue, and then kiss you.

Nowadays if you handed someone a clove-studded lemon (unless you were in a Martha Stewart craft class, where it would be seen as a sweet traditional curio), they would wonder what the hell you were doing.

To modernize this spell:

Buy a tin of Altoids cinnamon breath mints (cinnamon is an aphrodisiac), and enchant them before you give them to your desired one by kissing the box three times. In your mind's eye, see him take the box, pop a breath mint into his mouth, and lean over to kiss you. With this image firmly in your mind, whisper these words:

Kiss me kiss me, my heart's desire.
Place your lips on mine afire.

Now, in bewitchery you must work practically as well as magickally, so when you hand these enchanted Altoids to your beloved, make sure you are wearing something particularly fetching and that your lips are glossed with a strawberry lip gloss (another aphrodisiac) and that you are leaning toward him in an inviting way—lips quivering, eyes glistening—and I guarantee he will lean over and kiss you! Be aware that your lips really *will* be on fire—those cinnamon Altoids are hot!

> Bewitchers are focused and don't spread their magick too thin—i.e., no more than three guys bewitched at a time, or you may be behaving as badly as they do. You actually lower the probability of hitting your mark when you spray your bullets everywhere.

A BEWITCHMENT TO BLESS LOVE

This spell is called "The Vine and the Feather," and features two items potently aligned with love energy in many ancient spells as well as this more modern one.

The vine has always represented fidelity. In Victorian times, wedding bands were engraved with ivy, and newly married couples were given cuttings to plant by their front doors, to grow up and over the walls and bind the couple's love and passion to each other forever. The feather represents enlightenment, happiness, and freedom.

When the vine and the feather are used in magick together, they enchant the recipients of the spell with the power to love each other and yet not lose their identities. Independence and autonomy are essential components in a healthy, loving relationship.

So get some ivy (or any other creeping vine) and a feather. I like using black feathers (such as crow) because they represent the dark goddess—"dark" not meaning bad but meaning concentrated, unbridled female power. If you are partial to something pretty and pink like a parrot feather or to something more exotic like a peacock feather, that's equally perfect. In fact, I love peacock feathers. In old-school witchcraft they are seen as bad luck, but that is complete rubbish—I have had only good results charming men using peacock feathers.

Wind the ivy around one wrist and hold the feather in the same hand. Fan it toward the rising sun and say this incantation:

I bless our union
with strength and vigor,
light and passion
so love shall linger.

Tuck the vine and the feather in your purse, or make a cool fashion statement by wearing the vine and tucking the feather into your hair.

Get ready for some hot loving! And more important, long-term affection. The great thing about this spell is that it uses objects that represent freedom from boundaries—the sky's the limit for the love that can be expressed, and therefore, neither partner feels trapped. The guy won't realize he's been bewitched; he will just be having the time of his life and love will grow.

THE "MAKE HIM CALL" SPELL OR "I DON'T CARE ANYMORE" SPELL

This ritual is perfect for a situation where you have seen a guy a few times and had a great time, but you just don't know where you stand with him. And worse, deep down you suspect he is just not that honorable, but alas, you have fallen for him. This spell gives you back your power and a clear perspective on what is going on and if you want it to continue.

The best way to make him call is to reach that point where you just don't care whether he does or not anymore. This is easier said than done—except when you are employing bewitchery skills to amplify your resolve.

Bewitch a Man

You will need the following:

- Tablecloth or large piece of fabric
- Piece of paper
- Lead pencil
- Eraser
- The freedom to switch off your cell phone for eight hours
- Lots of candles

Spread out the cloth, light the candles around the room, and then sit in the center of the cloth with the paper, pencil, eraser, and your cell phone in front of you.

Write down why you want him to call.

Use the eraser to rub out the recorded reason, and blow the bits of rubber off the paper so they land on the cloth.

Write down all the self doubts you have as to why he hasn't called.

Rub them out and blow again.

And, finally, write down his name three times.

Rub it out and blow.

Pick up your cell phone and turn it off as you say these words emphatically:

I turn off the need in me.

Now put your cell phone away in a drawer. Scrunch up the paper and throw it out. Shake the eraser shavings off the cloth into the trash and throw the cloth in the wash.

Go and do something fun—you will be completely free of your desire for him to call.

Turn on your phone in eight hours. There will be a message from him. You don't believe me? Try it.

> Bewitchers *never* call—we just do a spell so that he calls us.
>
> Remember, casting a spell is like planting a seed: You don't keep digging it up to see how it's growing. You walk away and let the magick do its work. Go and do something fun that honors the hot, awesomely cool chick that you are. Believe in the power of the spells. He *will* call.

TWO MORE "MAKE HIM CALL" SPELLS

CALL ME 1

Look at your phone. Imagine the person you want to call picking up his phone or pulling his cell phone out of his pocket and dialing your number. Every ten minutes make this mental image. Don't attach an emotion to it. Just *know* that this event will happen. This does work. Just *know* it will.

This form of magick hinges on creating change with will. It works on sound principles of being aware of the power we have over our own destiny and that we create our world with our thoughts.

CALL ME 2

This is a short and sweet call-me spell that works fast—try it and see.

Write on a postage-stamp-size piece of paper the initials of the person you want to call you and place it under your home phone. Sprinkle herbs—dill, oregano, and caraway—around the phone in a clockwise direction as you picture the person picking up his phone and calling you.

Then say the following words:

Herbs of Mercury speed to me
the call I wish to receive.

Mercury is the planet of communication. The herbs you are using are aligned energetically with mercurial energy and will attract the results you need.

Remember: Don't be desperate as you do these "call me" spells. There is a big difference between fueling your magickal intent with your positive, empowered emotions and just being weak and desperate. Know that as a committed Bewitcher your magick will work. Cast your spell, get on with your day, and get out of your own way. Focus your energies elsewhere, and before you know it, the results will follow.

And if, despite your very best bewitchy attempts, there is no call within a time frame that is comfortable and appropriate for you, then know you have not failed but instead have been blessed—the universe has someone more wonderful than this guy in store for you.

THE "LITTLE CUPCAKE" SPELL

For sweet and sexy fun, this spell is great to do before you head out for a bewitching night on the town.

You will need the following:
- One pink candle—for love
- Your favorite-flavored cupcake—for yummy times

Bewitch a Man

Once gathered, light the candle and say these words:

My spell for love and fun has begun.

Eat the cupcake slowly, savoring its special treat. Visualize having a perfectly sweet and sexy time! Save some cupcake crumbs, and as you leave your house, sprinkle them on the earth as an offering to the Goddess, whispering these words three times:

Sexy and sweet—my spell is complete; tonight shall be a special treat!

HOW TO ENCHANT HIS BIRTHDAY CANDLES

This is the easiest bewitchery ever. Hold each candle to your heart and kiss it three times before placing it in his birthday cake as you say these words:

Your wish comes true
as does mine.
You shall adore me
for all time.

When he blows out the candles, he will be setting your enchantment in motion.

THE "FOUR THINGS THAT DEFINE HIM" SPELL

This spell works to attract a particular type of man into your life. It generally defines him through his career. So if your dream is to date a race car driver for thrills, a movie star for red-carpet openings, or a Wall Street investor for a big house and designer bags and shoes, this spell is for you.

For this spell you need four objects that are either literally near to him or symbolically relevant to him.

For example, if he is a race car driver, you could assemble these items:
- Model race car
- Piece of fireproof cloth (like their suits are made of)
- Piece of tire rubber
- Dirt from a racetrack that he has competed on

If he is a financial adviser, you could assemble these items:
- A twenty-dollar bill

Bewitch a Man

- Your bank statement with extra zeros added
- Copy of the stock market page from the *Wall Street Journal*
- His business card

Be creative in what you choose as the four things that define him. Try not to be a stalker as you go about getting the items, but definitely get things that relate to him and are close to his life.

Place them all in a box with a lid, and put the box under your bed. Every night before you go to sleep, open the box, touch each of the items, and then breathe into the box gently three times and say these words:

I breathe life into this union.
In you and me shall be love's fusion.
My will is great, its aim for good.
Come to me, as you should.

Place the lid back on, trapping your breath in the box. Take the necessary social steps to let him know of your interest. Bewitch, flirt, and always smile, and with this spell assisting you, you can be assured that victory shall be yours, and at the very least, you will get a hot date!

Such a simple spell that is only slightly devious! It will ignite the immediate potential for passion and love in the man that you desire. And it offers the added bonus of prettying up your home.

First, the slightly devious bit—you need to get some soil from the footprint of your desired one. How on earth are you going to accomplish this? Maybe appeal to his masculinity by parking your car on dirt and asking him to help you open the door because it seems to be stuck (of course, it isn't, so when he opens the car door, you can praise his strength immediately). But what you are really after is the soil from the imprint of his foot.

You also need to go to Pottery Barn or somewhere else where you can get a really lovely pot for the potted plant you will be preparing. The more effort you extend toward creating something of beauty as you conjure this spell, the more beauty your impending relationship will be blessed with.

The potted plant must be sweet basil that you should keep in a warm spot, protected from cold and too much direct sunlight. Water it well on hot days. From as far back as the ancient Romans, the scent of basil has been thought to inspire harmony of communication between lovers. In medieval times a young woman would place a pot of basil on her balcony or on her windowsill to let her suitor know that she would welcome his advances. It's your turn to tap into its power.

On the night of a full moon—preferably as it is rising—pot your gorgeous sweet basil and sprinkle the soil from his footprint around the base, pressing it in with your fingers gently as you say the following:

Love and passion grow fragrantly.
This man be mine and if not he
someone even more right for me.

BEWITCHERS NEVER SLEEP WITH A GUY THEY'VE BEWITCHED ON A FIRST DATE

American men are so different from European, British, and Australian men; in these countries if a guy and a girl like each other a lot and sleep with each other on the first date and the sex is good, they keep seeing each other! Duh! Doesn't that sound simple? But with most American men, if you sleep with them on the first night, you may never hear from them again. How ridiculous. But it is what it is. So hold off a little bit . . . unless, of course, you are using him for sex.

There is a great aspect to this spell if you read this incantation carefully. You have set your sights on your desired one because you think he is right for you—but you never know, underneath his flawless surface he may be a real jerk. This spell will nourish and grow in your life the great things that you recognized about him. Maybe someone even better for you will come along—a man who embodies the best of your desires and more. So water, nourish, and love the plant, and love will come within two full moons.

THE "CONJURE THE MAN YOU WILL MARRY" SPELL

To conjure the man who is perfect marriage material, you must believe you are the perfect marriage material yourself. So the first part of this spell is an "awaken to love within" ritual, followed by a "come to me, man of my dreams" conjuring.

For the first part of this spell, you will need these items:
- Seven white candles
- Sandalwood and frankincense incense sticks

Bewitch a Man

- Two roses
- Mirror

Sit naked in front of a mirror, surrounded by a circle of seven white candles for purity and spiritual enlightenment. Burn sticks of sandalwood and frankincense incense for wisdom and clarity. In each hand hold a rose—a symbol of love and female sexuality. Close your eyes, take a few deep breaths, and turn your awareness inward to a sense of inner peace. Concentrate on what qualities you desire in your life partner. When you have a clear vision and feel calm and ready, open your eyes and gaze at yourself in the mirror. Say the following:

I am worthy of love; I am worthy of grace.
Passion and fulfillment take their place
in my heart and in my mind.
My husband is now mine to find.

For the second half of this bewitchery you will need these items:
- Two red candles
- Piece of red paper
- Black ink pen

Now you will conjure the man of your dreams, a man you would marry in a heartbeat. Light the red candles knowing that one symbolizes you and one symbolizes your "partner to be." Write a description of the man you desire, but don't specify a particular person. This spell really does work best when you are not trying to interfere with another's free will but instead believe in every fiber of your being that the man you are about to describe is out there in the world for you. Close your eyes, concentrate, and visualize the qualities that you deeply desire in a life partner.

Here are some of my ideals that may inspire you:

- A man who adores me and makes me feel like a special treasure
- A man who calls me every day because he misses the sound of my voice
- A man who wakes before me and stays in bed watching me sleep and loving me
- A man who takes my hand and holds it to his heart when we are waiting for a table at a café
- A man who says every day how lucky he is to have me in his life
- A man who surprises me with flowers for no reason other than he loves me

When your list is finished, pluck three petals from each of the roses you used in the first part of your spell and place them upon your list. Using one of the red candles, drip drops of wax on the petals to seal them and your desire to the paper, as you say these words:

Come to me
man of my dreams.
As is my will
so must it be.

Fold the paper over so that the wax seals. Place this under your pillow. As you sleep, you will have visions of your future husband. Be on the lookout for him after this, because he will appear to you within fourteen days, and if you did your spell really well, you can expect to be married within the year.

> *"I have always loved any excuse to light candles, but abracadabra say what you will, within one month of casting Fiona's love spell, I met, fell in love with, and married my soul mate! Move over Glenda, Fiona is the true Good Witch of the West! There is no place like love!!"*
>
> —MINDY BURBANO, ACTRESS AND
> TELEVISION HOST

You have been girlfriend and boyfriend for a while, your family loves him, and his family loves you. You are so ready and he seems to be too, so why hasn't he proposed? The following spell will get things moving.

Pour a small glass of good red wine or pomegranate juice. Take two red roses and slip two gold rings over the stems, binding them together. You don't need to use expensive rings, but they have to look like wedding bands. Place the "wedded" roses on top of a photo of you and your boyfriend.

Take a wind-up clock and manually wind the hands faster and faster as you say these words:

Our love is blessed.
Time speeds up.
To wedded bliss
I raise my cup.

Place the clock down and drink the wine fast—gulp it down if you can.

Kiss the roses while your lips are wet.

Repeat the ritual the next night with two fresh

roses. Do this three nights in a row. The marital seed will be planted in his mind and a proposal will be imminent.

A SIMPLE AND SWEET LOVE SPELL

You can whip this one up in five minutes. You need to get a photo of your desired one. Please note this is one of those love spells that is potentially interfering with another's free will. Be nice and do this spell on someone who you know without a doubt is single and available for love as far you can possibly tell. And be *realistic*. It is best to cast this spell on someone you have already met who was friendly to you and whom you want to pull a little closer into your life to see if he is relationship worthy.

You will need these items:
- Bowl of honey
- One red candle that can stand in the bowl easily
- Picture of the person you want to be with
- One rose
- One teaspoon of basil

Light the candle while saying the person's name.

Place the picture in the bowl of honey. Sprinkle some basil over it. Place the rose in the honey, and say these words:

Love me, love me.
Our love will be
honey sweet.
Come to me.

Stick the candle, upright, into the bowl of honey, and let the candle eventually burn itself out. It is a good idea to plan this spell when you don't have to leave the house and can keep an eye on the flame.

When it has burned out, bury the bowl and everything in it, and say the following:

My spell is done with harm to none.

The one you desire shall make his interest known to you within seven days. Make sure you continue to bewitch him by being friendly, sexy, and confident, and do not tell him you cast a spell on him!

Bewitch a Man

THE "MAKE HIM FALL IN LOVE WITH YOU" SPELL (A TRADITIONAL SPELL WITH A BIT OF SEX HEX ADDED)

This is the kind of spell that you would offer a Gypsy silver to have her do for you in days of old. It is manipulative and interferes with another's free will, so I must include the appropriate warning.

To cast a spell over someone else for selfish purposes—that is, he has shown absolutely no interest in you despite some attempts on your part to garner his interest—is to risk invoking some nasty repercussions. But hey, every morning that we walk out of our house and get into the car to drive to work, we risk getting into a car accident. Does that stop us from going to work? No. We take the best precautions we can. We put on our seat belt, we drive carefully, and we minimize the risk. It's the same when doing a manipulative love spell. So if you attempt to make this guy fall for you, be prepared for those possible nasty repercussions. He may well fall for you, but you might find you're better off *without* his interest. Someone I know did a "come to me" spell like this, and it worked very well. They even married. Unfortunately, the guy turned out to be a bit of a psycho, and when she realized he was a nut job, she couldn't get rid of him and ended up very unhappy.

So, for the sake of being cosmically correct, I will say it is far better to do a general "come to me" spell than to specify a particular person. Focus on conjuring someone who embodies your preferred qualities and attributes—and let the universe decide who is best for you.

But . . . since I am sure you are still reading this only because you want someone specific, let us get started. The spell is a little complicated, but it can work very well if you are disciplined. Here's what you need to do:

Get hold of something that has his energy. Scoop soil from a footprint he has made, or perhaps procure some of his body bits—like hair or fingernails. (The girl I knew who did this spell offered her guy a manicure at work and he accepted; this would be really weird except that she worked in a hair salon as the manicurist, so it didn't seem too far-fetched.) Or even use saliva (a glass from which he has taken a sip works—just wipe a tissue around the rim to capture his essence and use that in the spell).

Prepare to concoct the spell by taking a bath,

adding half a cup of Epsom salts and five drops of lemon oil (or half a cup of the juice) to the water. Lemon and salt work to purify you and protect you from negativity; it's like putting on your seat belt when you get in your car.

Take a good soak, and as you lie in the bath, focus on your intent, picture the guy in your head, and say the mantra "*Come to me, come to me*" over and over. (Note: If you don't have a full bath, create a footbath— a low flat dish or even a foot spa that you can soak your feet in with the purification mixture added.)

When you are cleansed physically and spiritually, step out of the bath and towel yourself dry. Do the rest of this spell in an enclosed private place: It is a work in progress and you must not be disturbed.

Sprinkle a circle of salt and bring together a large red candle, a large plate, a foot-long piece of white cord, and "come to me" potent paste.

"COME TO ME" POTENT PASTE SPELL

Mix half a cup of water with cornstarch until it thickens. Add a teaspoon of damiana (for passion), a teaspoon of cinnamon (for potency), and six black peppercorns (for speedy results). Mix thoroughly, and then add drops of your own saliva procured from your tongue after you say his name three times.

Note: Damiana is a reasonably common herb with South American origins. It is used in lots of Santeria spells, and you can always get some from your local botanica. If you don't have a local botanica, order it on the Internet, or in a worst-case scenario, substitute crushed, dried rose petals—these are blessed by love but are not as strong an astral influence as damiana.

Carve his name into the candle, and then place it in the center of a large plate and sprinkle the body bits or soil that contains his energy around it. Take some of the paste and smear it over the carving of his name, keeping a clear vision of his face in your mind as you say these words:

Come to me, my will is great.
Now you can't escape your fate.

Take the white cord and trail it across your body, visualizing it absorbing your energy and your deep desire for him. Then wrap it around the base of the candle, tie it in a knot, and say the following:

Bewitch a Man

Bound to me, you now shall be.
As is my will, so must it be.

Light the candle flame and gaze at the flame as you intone these words:

Come to me, come to me.

When you have a clear vision of the two of you together, snuff the flame and say the following:

It is done.

Cover the candle and plate with a black cloth and leave. Every night for the next seven days, smear more paste on the candle, relight, and again chant the following:

Come to me, as is my will so must it be.

He will be yours within the week. If you are not satisfied with his degree of interest, do the spell again with a new candle and ingredients (you can reuse the body parts). You can do this spell for three weeks in a row. If he doesn't respond by then, give up and accept that the universe is doing you a favor because this person is really not right for you.

THE "BIND HIS LOVE TO YOU" SPELL

This is another love spell that potentially interferes with a man's free will. But to be honest, men rarely seem to know what they want—so give him a helping hand!

Find a black polished stone. (You will find stones like this at your local gardening store—the decorative ones used in feng shui gardens are perfect.)

When you have your stone, spit on your finger three times and rub into the stone. Now name the stone with the name of your desired one by chanting the following three times:

With all the strength of my desire,
I name you, [name of your desired one].

Now hold the stone to your heart, and using your greatest powers of visualization, see him walk toward you with his arms outstretched (literally "see" this happen in your mind's eye like it is playing out on a movie screen).

When this is clearly visualized, whisper these words into the stone:

Come to me, come to me.
Bound to me you must be
for the good of all, but mostly for me.

Place the stone in a small black box. (It is okay if the box has some subtle yet suitably potent decoration, especially red or gold—both are great power colors.) You can pick up good-quality cardboard boxes at any store with good gift-wrapping supplies.

Add to the stone personal objects that will reinforce the spell. For example, a squirt of your perfume on a piece of cloth, a hair you stole from his jacket when you were standing next to him at the water cooler, or even a picture of him.

Now place this love-binding spell box in a place where it will be seen by you frequently, as this will reinforce the spell every time you see the box. He will come to you—by walking straight up to you next time you see him, or the universe will create opportunities where you cross each other's path. It's up to you to seize these opportunities and approach him, knowing that he is bewitched and will respond favorably to your advances.

THE "REEL HIM IN" SPELL

This is another great attraction spell that sets the love wheels in motion and rolling straight toward you.

For this spell to work, you need to get a bit creative and do some writing. It's a particularly effective spell because you can't get away with repeating someone else's words and blanking out. You have to make up your own and keep it personal.

Some key points you need to include are:
- A description of the person you desire (again, preferably not a specific person—but if there is someone you completely desire, go for it)
- What you want to do with them when they are in your arms
- How long you want them for

Here is an example of something I wrote when I did this spell:

I call upon love that lingers.
He comes to me with sunshine and laughter.
Our love is blessed for good with passion
as I wind him closer, nearer and dearer.

Okay, so you have decided you really like what I have written and don't want to write your own stuff. That's fine. I give you permission to use my incantation, but you still have to interact in a sincere way with these words for them to work for you. So read them again and think about why they resonate with you. (And of course, if you want to write something better and more appropriate, go for it.)

When you have your charm written, get a stick that is large enough for you to carve a double heart into. You can use a sharp knife to do this—just don't cut your thumb off in your enthusiasm! A double heart means two hearts are joined as one.

Get some white ribbon. In most binding-love spells, red or black is used. But in this one, you want to invoke the spiritually pure energy of white because you want this spell to work for the good of all and for a higher evolved purpose. (Yeah right, you just want to shag him!)

Anyway, approach it as if you have a noble motive—and the more proud and profound you behave, the more effective this spell will be.

After you have traced your carving, kiss it three times and start to slowly wind the ribbon around the stick, chanting your invocation. Say it over and over, until you are lost in the words and the passion and pleasure they invoke as you know you are reeling in your desired one. When the ribbon is wound, blow on it three times to seal your intent, and place it under your bed. He will make his way to it before the next full moon.

If you tire of him, simply unwind the ribbon and you will break the spell. Easy come, easy go! (Well, that's the theory; you will have to try it to see for yourself.)

A NOTE ON TIMING OF

LOVE AND INFATUATION SPELLS

If you need to do any charming of love and passion, try to cast your bewitchery on a Friday (ruled by Venus, the planet of love) or during a new or full moon.

It is not essential but will give your magick an extra bump!

Bewitch a Man

Chapter Four

KEEPING THE SPARK

THIS NEW SET OF SPELLS FOCUSES ON TROUBLESHOOTING AND fixing problems in existing relationships as well as boosting weak starts so that love can blossom into something strong and fulfilling for the long term, for both of you.

THE "TIP THE ODDS IN YOUR FAVOR" SPELL

If you have been seeing someone for a couple of months, it's fair to want to know where the relationship is heading. Usually if it's not already clear, that's a bad sign—but there are situations where your initiating a welcoming (and bewitching) opportunity may tip the odds in favor of the relationship continuing and growing deeper rather than the fire going out.

Invite him over and have lots of candles lit. Before you light each one, kiss it and say these words:

True love will be revealed.

Carefully place these around your home or the room where you will spend time with your guy. Place some amethyst crystal on a nearby table to facilitate deep and honest communication. Finally, put on an item of clothing he has given you, or if he hasn't given you anything as a token of his affection (and if so, what the hell are you doing with him?), tuck a piece of paper that has his handwriting on it, or something else that is his, into your pocket (as long as it's not a dirty sock he left under your bed).

It's important as you enter into an event like this that you are very clear on what you will and won't accept. Sprinkle a little salt into your shoes or under the seat where you will sit when you initiate the conversation, to help your energy stay grounded and focused. If you want to be his girlfriend and be monogamous, then you need to make that clear and be ready for the possibility that he will say he doesn't feel the same way. But being armed with knowledge is far more powerful than wondering "what if?"

Be beautiful, charming, and friendly—but very honest about your needs. You are a Bewitcher, and as such, your needs come first. If you are with someone who is making you doubt yourself and your love worthiness and who you feel is giving you the runaround even a little bit, call him on it. With the bewitchery I described above working for you, I know you will get the answer you need—whether it brings joy or temporary disappointment—and you will move forward from this night with love and strength in your heart.

THE "OUR THOUGHTS CREATE OUR REALITY" SPELL

A girlfriend of mine was seeing a guy and it was going really well, but then it suddenly seemed to sour and she was ready to end it. She had been in a series of disappointing relationships (she lived in Hollywood and was dating flaky actors, which explains everything, really), but I encouraged her to try this spell before she took this drastic step, as I really felt their love had positive potential—*he* was a doctor, not an actor!

As overtaxed, love-exhausted modern women and

fledging Bewitchers, we can have the tendency to think negative thoughts and see a situation as far more dire than it actually is. Sometimes by rethinking a situation and revving it up with a little bewitchery, you can completely recharge all the best things about a relationship and get it back on track.

Make a plan to do something really special together and write it down. Fold the paper three times and put it in your bra, close to your heart. Leave it there for one full day. Every time your heart beats, you are charging up your intent to manifest a happy rebirth of your relationship. Invite him to the event and make it a surprise. If things have been a bit stale between you, I guarantee he will be thrilled to accept your surprise invite. Your special event could be an overnight trip to a casino to see a really great show or front-row seats at a hockey game—something that you know he will truly love and that you will take great pleasure in experiencing with him.

Know that you are offering this magickal event unconditionally. It is almost like you are creating a dream environment so that you can "dream up" a happier reality for the two of you. You have to know that your bewitching intent is more powerful than any negativity that you may feel is lurking in your connection with him.

Bewitch a Man

Don't see him for at least two days before the event. If you live together, find a reason to stay at a friend's or relative's house. You want to clear the air around you both and create a heightened sense of anticipation.

Now comes some bewitchery. Make sure you wear one item of clothing *inside out* on the date. It might be your undies, a stocking, or a watch or ring worn on the opposite hand. As you do this, you must state the following:

I reverse bad luck and welcome positive energy.

Bring with you your written plan, fully charged by your heartbeat, so that the night will go perfectly. If you do all this, there is a 99 percent chance that your relationship will be reborn positively and charged with great energy to move forward in an ever more fulfilling direction for both of you.

If despite your honest bewitching efforts, things don't get better, move on! Sometimes it is a greater show of positive strength to walk away than to stay.

Now you are probably wondering, did my girlfriend stay with the doctor? She did! By focusing on what was working between them, she created a positive, magickal environment. He came out of his "cave" and revealed that he was having a tough time at work and this had made him withdraw, and he appreciated her patience and support. They are now engaged!

"Not only is Fiona stunning, her pure, beautiful energy fills any room. The gift she shares with my audience is empowering, magickal, and from the heart—my listeners are captivated."

—TIFFANY GRANATH, HOST,
PLAYBOY RADIO'S AFTERNOON ADVICE

THE "COMPETITION FREEZE OFF" SPELL

As Bewitchers, we don't see our sisters as rivals, but that doesn't mean that sometimes they won't behave like rivals. When the situation just gets too blatant and awful (for example, you are wearing an engagement ring and she is still all over your fiancé at the office Christmas party), do this "Freeze Off" spell.

Write her name and her disagreeable action on a piece of paper. Wrap the paper around a piece of garlic, pour water over it in a small container, and freeze it at the back of the freezer. Leave it undisturbed.

"Fiona's "Freeze Off" spell worked like a charm for me. A while ago I met a girl at a nightclub and we became

friends. But as it turned out, she wasn't interested in a friendship with me; she was actually intent on stealing my boyfriend. After a month of hanging out with me and my boyfriend (we live together), she started really making my life miserable. She moved into an apartment on the same floor and was constantly knocking on our door; my guy would let her in, and she would make eyes and flirt with him. It was driving me crazy. He thought she was being friendly and that I was paranoid, and we even had a couple of fights about it. But this was her ploy. She was trying to drive a wedge between us. However, the day I did the "Freeze Off" spell, that evening she cornered him in the elevator of our building and tried to kiss him. It was then he realized that she really was trying to come between us. He rejected her and she moved out a few weeks later. But what was really odd was that I never saw her again. My boyfriend passed her in the hall a couple of times, and one night we were out at a club and my girlfriends said they saw her there; one even pointed her out to me, but when I turned to look, I couldn't see her. It was like she had become invisible in my life. I am sure it was because of the spell."

—KAREN, ACTRESS, HOLLYWOOD

THE "LOVE LETTER" SPELL

I created this very effective spell for a girlfriend. She was in one of those situations where she had been with a guy for over a year, and he would walk her dogs, had a key to her house, and let himself in whenever it suited him, and they had unprotected sex—yet he refused to call her his girlfriend. Rather than his familiarity breeding closeness, it bred contempt. He was judgmental and bossy, and she was not allowed to exert any demands on him. Their sex was great, and this certainly contributed to her being addicted to the imbalanced situation.

She tried to break up with him a number of times but kept getting sucked back into the same tired routine. She was not bewitching this man—she was enabling his crap and doing all women a disservice. After the hundredth phone call between us, analyzing her guy's behavior, I suggested she do this spell, as she deep down did not want to break up with him but knew that the status quo was unacceptable.

If your situation is like my friend's, try this spell.

You will need these items:
- Photo of yourself
- Black ribbon and red ribbon
- Pair of scissors
- Notepad and a pen

Bewitch a Man

Bind the ribbon around the photo. Acknowledge that this represents the way you are bound to the dysfunctional relationship.

Close your eyes and really connect with how this situation just can't go on anymore.

Open your eyes, pick up the pen, and say these words:

I am prepared to lose him if he will not meet my demands.

Now write your "non-boyfriend" (the boyfriend who treats you poorly more often than well) a love letter. Please note this is not a letter telling him about why you love him—but why you love yourself and how unless he changes, he is not going to be a part of your life anymore.

In my girlfriend's case, she wrote very specifically that after so long and with so much shared between them, she wanted to be told she was his girlfriend. She no longer wanted him letting himself into the apartment whenever it suited him. She required respect and needed him to work on his impatient and bossy nature. She wanted to be taken out on dates and treated like a princess. Like *his* princess. She wrote that if he wasn't prepared to do all this, it was completely over between them.

Now weave magickal intent into this act so that it will absolutely work to your favor whether he rises to the occasion, which will make you happy, or he doesn't and leaves, which will make you ultimately at peace because this spell will bless you with the confidence and strength to get over him rapidly.

Read the letter aloud, and then cut the ribbon binding your photo as you say these words:

I release the ties that bind me
no more tears shall blind me
only the best in this love shall greet me
or for now and evermore will leave me

Kiss your photo three times and put the letter and your photo in an envelope and mail it to him. Bury the ribbon deep in the regenerative earth to bury the current situation and allow a new one to develop. You will hear from him within three days, and the situation will be resolved in a way that will make you happy.

In my girlfriend's case, he said he did not want to leave her, and he was sorry his behavior had slipped so far in such a disrespectful way. He is now working on himself and treating her like the princess that she is.

Bewitch a Man

POWER OF THREE

Often you will see the number three used in my spells. Since ancient times this number has been seen as sacred and empowered with an ability to multiply and magnify the intent of any spell and ritual. Bewitchery is mostly based on Celtic and Northern European shamanic magick, and the number three was then considered a supreme number of manifestation. When the science of mathematics became commonplace in the sixteen hundreds, it confirmed the Celts were justified in their choice of three as a magickal number. When three is multiplied by itself to become nine, it becomes a number that can always come back to itself, representing a creative power and complete magickal energy circuit.

Sample equation: 3 x 3 = 9, and then multiply any number by 9 and it will return to nine—for example, 8 x 9 = 72, and 7 + 2 = 9. Or 2 x 9 =18, and 1 + 8 = 9.

So do something magickal three times, and nine times more magick will come back to you!

THE "BRING MY LOVER BACK" SPELL

Another girlfriend of mine was in a roller-coaster relationship. During happy times we used to laugh together and say, "Hey, it's more exciting than a merry-go-round." But it often was very draining for her (and me also, to be honest, as I counseled her), and after a while she felt the lows exceeded the highs, and like a good empowered Bewitcher, broke up with him.

Two months passed and she dated other guys but missed him terribly. She started to look at herself and how she could have behaved better in their relationship, and then one day she came to me and said, "I want him back. I want to give our love another chance." I was impressed with the work she had done on herself, so I gave her the following spell to do. It is very powerful and based on an old voodoo charm that is benevolent in nature. But beware: If your relationship was bad because he treated you badly, then you are only going to get three times the abuse if you bewitch him back. If you were being a bitch to him, then you need to work on yourself to be worthy of his love—or you will suffer karmic fallout in other areas of your life.

The "Bring My Lover Back" spell works on the love and affections between two people and weakens the barriers causing you to be apart. It only helps repair when you were in a good relationship that went awry. It does not work if you were never really close. It also won't work if you do any of the following: relentlessly call and e-mail him, stalk him, or create drama. Once you do this spell, you have to trust the process and just let it do its work on the spiritual and magickal plane.

You will need to make a doll that represents the person you want to bring back. You can get some cloth and cut it into the shape of a doll and sew it together, or if that is too hard, buy a Ken doll or something. It basically needs to be a human male shape. To personalize it, you can either write his name on it or, if you still have some of his clothing, cut off a little piece of the cloth and wrap it around the doll.

You also need some dried herbs that are enchanted to bring back love.

A self-made bundle of dried vervain, sage, and bay leaves, wound tightly with cotton cord, will work best. But if you are having trouble getting a hold of these, go to a New Age store and buy a stick of white sage leaves bound together, which American Indians use for smudging and purifying. The heavy, sacred smoke is what you will be using as a part of your spell.

At midnight (the most bewitching of all hours) light four white candles and place them on a table in the directions of north, south, east, and west (or as close as you can approximate).

Place the doll on a plate in the center and sprinkle a circle of salt around it, throwing some over your left shoulder as you do this, for luck and protection.

Place your hand over the doll and say the following:

I name thee [name of person you want back in your life].

Pick up the doll and blow three long, slow breaths over its mouth and say these words:

I breathe life into thee, and into our love, come back to me, come back to me

Now carefully light the incense bundle and fan the smoke over the doll, saying the following solemnly:

In the name of good my spell is cast.
It is my intent to cause no harm
but my will is strong and its action swift.
Come back now as is my wish.

Keep fanning the smoke over the doll, knowing that it is like a smoke signal that your love will recognize and respond to.

Make sure you finish the spell within eleven minutes: snuff the incense into dirt to make sure it is completely out, place it and the doll into a shoe box or similar box, and place the box under your bed.

He will be back in your life within seven days. What you do with this opportunity is up to you.

WHY ELEVEN?

Eleven is a number that is aligned with illumination of the spirit, awareness of knowledge, and an understanding of personal power that is beyond the grasp of the average person (read: non-Bewitcher). It invokes qualities that are intuitive and visionary and promotes success in any undertaking.

THE "I NEED A MAN" SPELL

We strong, beautiful, bold Bewitchers can sometimes intimidate men, and the following spell is wonderful for those of us who need help relinquishing control. The goal is to appear deceptively more helpless and of an archetypal feminine energy so that we don't threaten their delicate male egos. They will feel like they have something they can offer us.

You can do this spell anytime, but it is particularly good to do it every morning for a few days leading up to a date or to some significant time you will be spending together.

Dress in white and place some white, scented blossoms in your hair. Gaze at yourself in the mirror. Say these words with heartfelt energy:

I am a maiden pure and sweet.
I let this man sweep me off my feet.
I open my arms to love and blessings
new and pure without expectations.
He fills me.
He nourishes me.
He shows me more
than I can see.

If wearing white and flowers in your hair is not appropriate when you see him, wear a token of your maiden innocence. A sweet, fresh gardenia in your hair, a white silk scarf at your throat, a white blouse, or even just spotless white underwear, is perfectly acceptable. When you adorn yourself in white, you do it with the intent to release control and allow him to assert himself in your life. And when you are with him, let him control the conversation. Always direct your attention back to him—his opinions, his experiences, and his actions. Smile and let him be, and he may surprise you and tell you something you don't already know!

THE "SHARE HIS PASSIONS" SPELL

Sometimes, to keep the love alive, you need to find joy in unlikely diversions. I had to perfect this spell quite a few years ago when I was dating a football player. Even though I had always had an aversion to contact sports and the frat-boy mentality that accompanies such sports, I nonetheless had fallen hopelessly in love. What to do? To make matters worse, he was also a meat eater and I was an avowed vegan. I didn't even wear leather! And while he loved beer, the smell of it made me sick. But he had the biggest, most genuine smile and a truly good heart—plus the sexiest legs I had ever seen. So I fell in love with him and ended up creating the drinking-beer-and-eating-burgers spell.

Do this spell on the morning of your Super Bowl

date, or whatever activity you are about to be inflicted with in the name of bonding with him.

You will need these items:
- One orange candle (orange is for enthusiasm)
- Olive oil (for ease of communication and action)
- Photo of the appropriate contact sport (easily printed off the Internet or taken from a magazine)

Carve your bewitched one's initials into one side of the candle and yours into the other. Rub a little olive oil over the carvings as you say the following:

Smooth and easy
our time shall be.
Fun and laughter
bewitched by me.

Place the candle over the photo and light it, smiling as you do so. Gaze at the flame and picture you and your guy laughing, eating burgers and drinking beer at the pub, and having a great time. Hell, picture his team winning while you are at it, and if your

Bewitcher skills are well honed, no doubt they will win. It will be win-win situations all around. You will be able to tolerate the frat-boy environment and even lighten up enough to enjoy yourself too. Who knows, you may actually become a burger-eating, beer-drinking contact-sports fan (like I have!).

Chapter Five

ℒive ℒike a ℬewitcher

BEING A BEWITCHER IS NOT JUST ABOUT CASTING spells and having a positive attitude. It's about how you *live*. Your life choices are an essential part of your magick. The objects you surround yourself with, the situations you place yourself in, and how you choose to look can strengthen your power and bewitchery over men. When you become a really adept Bewitcher, you realize that you are not practicing magick, you are *living* it. A newfound sense of personal power and self-esteem is projected from within you and reflected upon the world around you.

After doing all the inner work, it is important to be "framed" in the most flattering of ways.

A Bewitcher will benefit greatly by having a BBC in her home. It is a "magickal hot spot" that you create in your environment as a visual and energetic affirmation of your bewitching intent. Meditating at it, doing spells near it, or even simply looking at it can help you focus and connect with your bewitching powers. Your BBC can be as elaborate or minimal as you prefer, and it should reflect your personal taste and energy in such a way that pleases and empowers you.

Choose an area of your home that you can devote to your BBC. It can be an entire room, a table or dresser top, or even just a windowsill. It needs to be somewhere accessible for you but also private enough so that you feel it is your special, sacred place.

You need to have the four elements of natural power honored and represented:
- Fire = Candle
- Air = Incense
- Earth = A crystal
- Water = Bowl of regularly changed water with a small seashell or pinch of salt in it (for purity and to represent the ocean)

You also need to have yourself honored as a divine Goddess Bewitcher in your BBC, so include your favorite picture of yourself.

Further ideas to decorate your BBC include:
- A lovely vase of fresh flowers or a living plant to honor the natural world of which you are a miraculous part
- Ornaments or artwork that remind you of all the magick and beauty there is to enjoy in the world

I recommend that every morning you perform this short ritual to affirm your bewitching life path and turn on your "man-magnet" energy.

The BBC morning ritual consists of these acts:
- Light the candle, burn a little incense, and fan it with your hand
- Pick up the crystal and hold it to your heart
- Stir the water with your finger in a sunwise (clockwise) direction
- Gaze at your picture, blow yourself a kiss, and say, *I am a goddess!*

I guarantee every day will start fantastically!

Bewitchers always look hot, not only because they are totally in touch with their inner beauty but because they know how to dress to impress and get what they want—exactly when they want it. The best way to dress as a powerful Bewitcher is to always dress to please yourself, and that will confer a powerful magick that will bewitch any man.

BEWITCHING DRESS CHECKLIST

The following dress guidelines are inspired by one of the most bewitching women ever seen on the big screen—Kim Novak in the pre-*Bewitched* classic, *Bell, Book and Candle*. If you haven't seen this movie, buy it on Amazon or keep an eye on the classic-movie cable channels. Kim is strong, independent, and extremely bewitchy. She showcases extreme classic style and absolute sexiness. Enjoy experimenting with some or all of the suggestions below, with the intent of exploring and evolving your personal style to reflect your growing Bewitcher status.

1. Wear skirts in smooth fabrics, slim cut and tapered at or just above the knee, with a belt to accent the waistline and honor a curvy goddess shape.

2. Deep V-neck lines celebrate the lush, fertile

beauty that only a woman can have.

3. High heels are the classic Bewitchers' shoes. Be seductive and strong as you walk slowly in them, and leave the rat race behind as you savor the stir that you create in the men around you.

4. Panty hose are not good for Bewitchers, as convenient as they may seem to be. They allow for no ventilation or freedom of movement, creating discomfort in an area that should feel only pleasure—our sacred sex. Instead, the classic seamed stocking is very flattering. Skin-toned stockings can be even more tantalizing than black, which can look too gothic and heavy—often great on the catwalk but not that sexy for the average guy (and remember, all guys are average compared to us; never put them on a pedestal!).

5. Makeup should make you look like you just had sex. Flushed and fresh, with smoky eyes and moist lips—but subtle and sexy. A good tip is to highlight either eyes or lips. Never both.

6. Bewitching calls for manicures and pedicures, smooth legs, fresh sweet-smelling hair, and subtle but potent perfume that enhances your own natural pheromones. If you don't have a signature scent, go and get a bunch of samples and wear a different one

every day. Whichever one gets you the most compli-
ments from men will become your signature scent.

7. The most important accessory a Bewitcher can
   have is her smile—highlighted with a sexy giggle
   or a happy laugh.

A BEWITCHING BEAUTY TIP

A Bewitcher's eyes can be her most powerful
weapon of seduction. To give your gaze supernatural
powers, use a light concealer under your eyes to
play down any dark circles. Do a smoky, sexy eye
shadow, and then highlight the inner corner of
your eyelids with a hint of silvery-metallic,
moonlight-sheen shadow. Now apply some dark
eyeliner along the base of your upper-lid eyelashes,
and to enhance your magnetically mysterious look,
flick the outer edge in an upward direction. Use an
eyelash curler before applying a few coats of dark
mascara, as seductive, curvy, full lashes will
complete your luscious, lusty look.

BEWITCHYLICIOUS GLAMORIZATION

When you head out, and you want to make a big visual
impact, keep your outerwear chic and simple, but
underneath, wear luscious underwear to make you feel
and radiate sexy energy. Be sure to wear one piece of

opulent jewelry that visually states your power. Stones of topaz, sapphire, and ruby can make a sensual impact and since ancient times have been renowned for their seductive powers. Once you are dressed, accessorized, and looking amazing, perform this spell to even further enhance your magnetism for men.

Stand in the center of four lit red candles that have been anointed with cinnamon oil. You need to invoke the blessings of the erotic guardians of the night. Close your eyes, raise your arms in the air, and call out these words:

Guardians of the night
behold me in your exotic light
so I shall bewitch all at my sight.

In your mind's eye see the four candle flames leap up and join above your head, spiraling into the cosmos, and know that you are the center of all beauty and glamour in the universe as the guardians bless and carry you on their wings of exotic desire.

Of course, once you've conjured your man and bewitched him and he is fascinated not only by your body (which is always the first port of call for his attention) but also by your mind and spirit, you can start preening and prancing around in front of him in all your finery. He will enjoy your performance and celebrate your great creative spirit and the pride you take in adorning yourself.

But to get him to start falling under your spell in the first place, practice KISS (Keep It Simple, Sorceress) and use some age-old femme fatale techniques combined with reverse psychology. The following are some absolute no-fail ways to attract him and two appropriate places to experiment with your early bewitching dress skills.

AT THE SUPERMARKET

Everyone else at the supermarket usually looks like they just got out of bed, so this is a prime place to stand out.

A split skirt is much more bewitching than a mini (Bewitchers know it's all about the tease and the glimpse of that stairway to heaven). If you don't think your thighs are split worthy, immediately turn to the "Thou Shalt Love Thyself—No Matter What!" ritual (page 115), and then highlight another asset—your breasts. If your bottom half is bootylicious, then your top half is likely to be also.

Position your arms on the shopping cart so that as you slowly strut around the supermarket you are squeezing your breasts together, creating a superinviting little advertisement of the cornucopia of your personal delights. If you don't have ample lumps in the front, go to Victoria's Secret and buy one of their *amazing* push-up bras (and the matching undies while you're at it—remember the Bewitchers' Rule: Deep down, where it counts, we are into making ourselves feel good as much and as often as possible and that includes wearing supernice undies all the time).

So, does strutting around the supermarket in a split skirt and with boobs pushed together sound ridiculous? Absolutely! But guys are simple creatures, who will be more than happy to help you with your produce.

LAVENDER LUCK

To add to your obvious physical charms, spruce up the magick by tucking a piece of lavender into your bra. This is aligned with a medieval love charm where a girl would tuck a piece of lavender into her buttonhole over her heart to attract a man.

AT THE NIGHTCLUB

Where everyone else is pumped up to the elevens, with all their seductive feathers of finery on display, what does a Bewitcher do? She dresses down, down, down (which is what she'll be saying to the all the guys trying to hump her leg as she perches on her bar stool).

Don't be misled. There is an *art* to looking like you don't care about impressing anyone. Once again, think,

Bewitch a Man

"How would Angelina Jolie look?" Tousled hair that looks like she just got out of bed after a fantastic shag. We are not talking about a greasy bird's nest here—but rather about something that smells sweet and feels soft and yet is a bit messy. Add a black T-shirt, black pants, and pointy-toe flats, and you have an outfit that's chic, comfortable, confident, and very bewitchy. It's a great Bewitcher's skill to never look like you're trying to impress anyone except yourself.

When you are dressed down, it's essential that your energy is up! A big bright smile and glossy inviting lips will have guys tripping over themselves to get closer to that bewitching energy that you exude.

Dressing as a Bewitcher is easier than choosing among the 166+ choices *InStyle* magazine offers every month. Dress like a woman. Dress like a feminist by celebrating the feminine. Try dressing as a Bewitcher for a day—even just as an experiment— and watch every man fall at your feet.

I realize that sometimes, if we are feeling a bit flat (or fat) and low on self-esteem, we don't always make the best choices in how we present ourselves to the rest of the world. I know I will always gravitate toward dull sweats and baggy shirts when I am not feeling very bewitchy. But one of the best ways to perk yourself up into your power again is to know the power inherent in dressing like a Bewitcher. And that means looking magnificent—confident in whatever you are wearing.

The following are more important than food—so if you must choose between Whole Foods and Sephora, choose Sephora every time. Besides, you won't need food in the house because men will be constantly taking you out to dinner.

- Your favorite fruity body lotions
- Fresh flowers
- Scented candles
- Frothy body scrubs
- Lush creamy face moisturizer
- New undies and push-up bras
- Fun new sex toys

Anything else that makes you feel self-indulgent and pampered

In bewitchery, "good looks" are not necessary—but looking good is. A powerful Bewitcher is always compelling—whatever her shape, hair color, or physical features. Bewitchers know that if they don't fit what society defines as mainstream attractive, it is really only a positive for them. This gives them room to stand out and be different from everyone else, and combined with self-respect and self-adoration, makes them utterly compelling.

Bewitch a Man

For a Bewitcher, goddessliness is next to cleanliness. Here are a few tips to make bath time an extremely pleasant experience, either alone or with company.

GYPSY-BEWITCHER LOVE SALTS

Make these for yourself and soak in the bath regularly to increase your love-attraction qualities.

You will need these items:
- Half cup of rock salt
- One cup of Epsom salts
- Half cup of coconut oil
- Five drops of ylang-ylang oil
- Two handfuls of gardenia petals (or similar white flower, like jasmine, rose, or scented lily)

Place the salts and oils in a plastic bag and hold the open end tightly closed, and gently shake as you say this charm:

Love, love, love
comes to me
sweetly as it pleases me.

Pour the salts into the bath and swirl the water in a sunwise direction to disperse them. Float the flower petals on the surface and sink into the tub, continuing to repeat the charm at least a few more times—the more the better. The added bonus is that your skin will be beautifully soft from these salts, so any man who touches you will be transfixed by how good you feel.

HEIGHTEN YOUR SEX DRIVE

Ensure you will always feel sexy by blending the appropriate oils together and mixing them into a warm bath. You can do this for your man as well. Don't be afraid of slipping into the bath with him, as those oils will be sexy for you, too. However, if he gets into your bath, he may just feel sleepy! The oils that arouse you will have the opposite effect on him!

For women: Regular bathing in a warm bath with several drops each of the essential oils of rose, clary sage, and basil will balance your moods, soften your skin, and allow you to give full rein to your sensuality. For simplicity and ease, I suggest buying Jurlique's "Wise Woman Blend" (www.jurlique.com), as it is a beautiful concoction of the right oils.

For men: Regular bathing in a warm bath with several drops each of cypress and patchouli and cinnamon

Bewitch a Man

will unleash the god in him. Again, Jurlique has beauti-fully pure, organic essential oils, and it is worth invest-ing in these individual oils so you can mix a potent blend for your man.

This divine and silky smooth bath is perfect to nour-ish a couple physically and spiritually and to encour-age love to blossom and grow.

You will need these items:
- Six cups of organic milk
- Twenty-two drops of ylang-ylang oil, or you could try Jurlique's "Romance Blend," which features ylang-ylang along with patchouli and orange for an intoxicating, lovely, "scentual" experience!

As you run the bath, stir the milk and oil together in the warm water with your hand in a sunwise direc-tion, visualizing as you do, your man falling (or stay-ing) deeply in love with you.

To give your magickal intent even more power, hold a pink rose quartz crystal loosely in your hand as you stir the water. Know that rose quartz is energeti-cally aligned to pure unconditional love. It may be practical to keep a rose quartz crystal in a special container by the bath to use repeatedly for this purpose. Too much love is not enough, I say!

You can further enhance the experience of your love bath by lighting red candles, floating rose petals on the surface of the bath, and burning incense of vanilla or a similar luscious tropical scent.

SWEETWATER BATHING POTION

It's common to wash your body in the bath or shower, but this Sweetwater bathing potion actually cleanses your heart. The herbs are chosen for their energetic resonance aligned with your heart's happiness.

You will need the following ingredients (if you are using dried herbs instead of fresh, use half a handful instead):

- One handful of heartsease (wild pansy—grows fresh in the springtime across America, but you can buy it dried from health stores)
- One handful of passionflower (a lovely vine that has large white flowers with purple centers—its calming effect is traditionally used as a cure for insomnia)
- One handful of rosemary (the original name

Bewitch a Man

is derived from Latin meaning "dew of the sea," which is why it is used in Sweetwater, as it represents the blessings of Mother Ocean and all her abundance of good things)

- One handful of peppermint (to freshen you and get you ready for lots of good lovin')
- Quarter cup of pure vodka (No, don't drink it! It cleanses negative energy when used on the exterior, not interior)
- Eight ounces of springwater (for purity)

Soak the herbs in the water and vodka (which have been stirred together in a large covered pot) for at least twenty-four hours. Do not heat. Strain the mixture and put the liquid in a container with a rose quartz crystal added for one more night.

Now the Sweetwater is ready to use. After a regular bath take one cup and slowly pour down over your heart from throat height. Breathe deeply and in your mind's eye see your heart chakra pulse a clear green light (its purest color).

Keep the Sweetwater covered and in a dark, cool cupboard for up to one week. Any longer and it has to be refrigerated, which will certainly be chilly if you use it, but is fine if you are comfortable with that.

BEWITCHER DAILY DIARY

Begin each day with a boost!

1. Wake up, stretch, go to the mirror, and smile at yourself, saying, "Good morning, beautiful!"
2. Put a little water in your mouth and splash your face twelve times with your eyes open (its an ancient yogic way of clearing your thoughts and enhancing positive energy in the body).
3. Go to your Bewitcher Base Camp and light candles and incense, and state a positive intent for the day.
4. Do some exercise.
5. Shower and get dressed, taking care to honor and compliment the stunning Bewitcher that you are.
6. Put on your power-charm bracelet, necklace, or whatever your empowered love amulet is.
7. Eat something healthy for breakfast. (This one can of course be done as soon as you are hungry, in between any of the above events!)

Have a bewitching day!

Bewitch a Man

Chapter Six

LOVE THE ONE YOU'RE WITH

TO BE ABLE TO BEWITCH A MAN YOU HAVE TO START with a clean inner slate and let go of any residue of sadness and anger that you may harbor toward the opposite sex. You must be able to see men as friends—no matter how embittered you are after the appalling way men have treated you or your girl-friends in the past. Bewitchers know we create our reality with our thoughts—the way we view the world is how it manifests.

The first step in letting go is taking responsibility for our situation—at least partially, anyway. When men treat us badly there is a portion of us that enables and allows that to happen. By taking responsibility, you take control and become empowered. That is the cornerstone of bewitchery.

The following rituals are great ways to clean, clear, and connect with your true needs—without emotional baggage. When you know what your needs really are, you can get them satisfied.

THE "LET IT GO" RITUAL

The best time to do this ritual is at sunset. As the sun sinks over the horizon, visualize it taking away that which no longer serves you in your goal to bewitch not just any man but the *right* man.

The ritual is simple. All you need to do is the following:
- Write a list of what you need to let go of.
- Burn it.
- Bury the ashes somewhere away from where you live, and walk away without looking back.

Remember what makes our actions magickal and transformational is the intent with which we fuel them, so know as you write your list that you are working with a couple of powerful magickal elements—fire and earth. Fire purges and earth regenerates—so when you burn your list, you purge those things from your life, and the earth will make sure they don't come back, and will, instead, allow new, more positive experiences to flourish and grow in your life.

Here is what happened when I performed my "Let It Go" ritual. I went to the top of a canyon in the Hollywood Hills (it was all I could do at the time not to throw myself off it—I was so desperately unhappy) with my notepad and my pen and a packet of matches. (I checked first that there was no fire warning and no wind that day.)

I sat there thinking for an hour as I watched the sun get lower in the sky, and then I wrote my heart out. I remembered awful things that guys had done to me as far back as when I was twelve, when I was just awakening to my sexuality. I remembered how a boy I had had a crush on spit in my face (literally); how my first boyfriend, with whom I had my first sexual experience, commented on how ugly my labia were; and how I had endured years of emotional, mental, and even physical abuse from the losers I had fallen in love with.

It was a really long list, and it took another hour to write it. I capped it all off with the most recent experience at the time—a guy who I really thought was going to be a significant part of my mature life. It hurt me deeply when it was revealed that despite this guy's parading himself as a mature loving man ready for a serious relationship, he was actually a liar. He had come on like a freight train and swept me off my feet—complimenting me, being sweet, and even taking me to meet his mother—but then three months into it he told me he didn't consider us boyfriend and girlfriend and he wanted to date other girls.

At such a poignant point in my life, the turn this relationship took was brutally painful and distressing. I cried and cried as I wrote the last part of my list, and my tears made the ink on the paper blur. The sun was setting. I set fire to the list of grievances as the last ember of the sun's rays dispersed into a soft pink glow coating the western sky. When all that was left was a big pile of ashes, I turned them into the ground with a stick and walked to my car without looking back.

I felt really peaceful but emotionally drained, and I went to bed as soon as I got home, and had a dreamless, deep sleep. The next morning I got up early and went to my spin class, and it was during the class that I had the following revelation . . .

As Pat Benatar so eloquently put it in the eighties, "love is a battlefield." Injury, heartache, and heartbreak

Bewitch a Man

are inevitable—whether you are single and trying to find love or in a marriage of ten years that has hit rocky times. What isn't inevitable is getting better and stronger through each experience. That's something the individual has to decide to do on her own.

As I sat there spinning, I realized all those torturous, devastative thoughts that I had been crying myself to sleep over for the past month were gone, completely gone. The mixed messages this guy had been giving and the ultimate betrayal and disrespect he had inflicted on me were things of the past. I realized I had survived this heartbreak. I then saw my love life not as a string of failures, but as a string of successes! I saw how rather than getting beaten down when I went into battle, I came out stronger and wiser every time. I was a survivor.

And this awareness suffused every fiber of my being. As the blood pumped through my veins, the sweat poured out of me, and the adrenalin flooded my body, I fell completely in love with what a cool, awesome human being I was. And it was in that moment, I knew I deserved to be loved by the right man. And knowing that was a profound magick unto itself. I knew that there was nothing wrong with me—except that I had been aiming too low.

The "Let It Go" ritual can help clear the dust so that

you can see yourself and celebrate yourself. It will help you set your sights on the best targets, the ones that will nourish and enrich your life—not the ones that are just going to drag you backward into the swamp with them.

And by the way, two months after I broke up with the guy, he text messaged me and said he missed me and wanted me back! Needless to say, I didn't take him up on the offer—I had completely moved on and into my own power.

SIMPLE METHODS AND SPELLS TO HELP HEAL SADNESS AND DEPRESSION (AND EMBRACE THE HAPPIER TIMES)

Try an aromatherapy oil blend based on the divinely euphoric essential oil of clary sage. Jurlique's "Tranquility Blend" is perfect for this. (Please note: If you are pregnant, clary sage is contraindicated, so use an oil featuring geranium, like Jurlique's "Pampering Blend.")

Drink tansy tea, a yummy coffee substitute available at health food stores. Tansy honors the goddess within and represents the immortal and eternally renewing qualities of life. Drink it with honey to add sweetness to your spirits.

Take Saint-John's-wort, tablets or tincture. Nicolas

Culpepper (a renowned elder herbalist) recommended steeping the herb in wine and drinking a glass before bed to prevent bad dreams and free the heart from sorrow.

THE "RELEASE SADNESS" SPELL

You will need these items:
- One slim piece of oak, gum, or maple wood (all excellent conductors of energy)
- One white rose
- Sea salt

Stand under the sky somewhere private and beautiful. Sprinkle a circle of salt around you and kneel, plunging the stick into the earth in front of you, holding the other end in both hands. Channel your feelings of sadness and depression through the wood, and if you cry, let your tears fall onto the earth. Say these words:

I release pain and woe.
From me all sadness flows.
Heal my heart, Mother Earth,
so I am free of fear and hurt.

Take the stick out of the earth and place the white rose there and say the following:

I am what I am, and what I am has beauty and strength. I offer this rose as a symbol of the beauty and love that will grow again in my heart and my life.

Thank the earth for helping you and kiss it three times. Remain seated in your sacred earth circle and allow yourself to feel peaceful and free. Love and joy will start to enter your life in great abundance from this moment onward.

POWER OF CIRCLES

Bewitchers love circles as they do stars—circles protect and stars empower. Just as the star shape can confer ancient talismanic protection and power, so can the circle. Anytime you surround either yourself or an object with a circle, whether it be literally (for example, sprinkling salt or flower petals around a picture of your new boyfriend) or imaginatively (for example, visualizing a circle of pink light around your bed before making love with your partner there), you are creating a protected and pure space so that only good things can take place within.

Bewitch a Man

You will need the following:

- Pink notebook
- Pink pen
- A day to people watch (that is, girl watch)
- Pink candle

The best time to do this is on a sunny day when there are lots of girls out and about.

The best place to do this is at a shopping mall, beach, popular park, or art gallery.

To start the spell, sit somewhere really comfortable where you can girl watch. Start making notes in your pink book about how lovely the girls you see are. Rather than looking at girls as competition—fat, skinny, well dressed, badly dressed, and so on—write two really nice things about each girl. It may be that she has a lovely smile, glossy hair, a great pep to her step, elegant hands, or she simply exudes positive, wonderful energy. She may appear to you as a loving mother, a great friend, or a pillar of strength.

Fill your book with notes on how lovely and amazing your fellow sisters are and be as prolific as you feel moved to be.

Finish the spell in your bedroom by lighting the

pink candle, and by its love light, read everything you wrote down. Now hold your pink book to your heart and say this invocation:

All that I can perceive
is a reflection of what is part of me:
Love and light and perfect beauty
within my heart and all around me.

Know that all the wonderful things you acknowledged in your sisters were recognizable to you because they are all a part of you. (If you were unable to write anything nice in your pink book, you need to do some serious work on yourself—I would suggest reading the "Thou Shalt Love Thyself—No Matter What!" ritual on page 115 and the "Your Sisters Are Not Your Rivals" ritual on page 201.)

Kiss your pink book three times and place it next to the candle, sprinkling a little salt in a circle around both. The salt circle will seal the energy invoked by your spell so that as you sleep, it will infuse your aura with radiant, unconditional beauty.

Watch men respond to your bewitching radiance the next day. And something else really nice will happen—your fellow sisters will respond to your friendly and appreciative energy too. The more happy sisters there are out there, the happier you will be as you all tune into one another's positive collective consciousness.

Remember, Bewitchers share the love!

POETRY IN MOTION

Lines of poetry, or if you are not so gifted, favorite lines from a song that speaks to you of bewitchery and enchanting the man of your dreams, can infuse your aura with positive empowering energy.

Write little pieces of poetry or song lyrics to yourself about how wonderful you are and how you are going to bewitch the man of your dreams. Spray your words with your favorite perfume and tuck them into your shoes, into your pocket, under your pillow, in your bra. Read or sing them out loud as you spray them and tuck them into your world around you, visualizing in your mind's eye that you are like a divine little spider spinning a web of enchantment around you to support your efforts in bewitching the man of your dreams. Weave this web of positive enchantment around you as much as you like.

This spell is inspired by a long conversation I had with a girlfriend who had been divorced for a couple of years but had not met anyone who could heal the damage in her heart done by her ex-husband. She was crying and saying she just could not face doing the "dating" thing anymore and that going back out into the world of "single girls on a meat rack" was so belittling and draining. As she kept saying the "date" word, it really hit me just what an awful word it is. I suggested that we banish this horrible word that carries with it so much negative energy—the baggage of so many people who terminally "date" but never find lasting fulfillment and happiness. The whole dating thing in the USA is really just set up for men to be able to have their cake and eat it too. I can't stand dating someone and knowing that I am just filling in time while they shop around for something potentially better.

My girlfriend and I both agreed we could not enable this juvenile situation between the adults of our species anymore. We decided to banish the *d* word with the following ritual.

You will need the following:
- Piece of white paper about three inches square

- Black marker pen
- Cut clove of garlic (to banish and purify)
- A stone
- Small shovel
- Some dirt

Pick up the black marker and write in big capital letters the following:

D A T E

Using the garlic, trace over the letters with a big X, and then blow on it three times as if you were blowing the letters away.

Fold the paper over and take it outside. Dig a hole, place the paper at the bottom and the stone on top so that this word and all it represents will never raise its head in your life again.

From that moment on, do not ever say the *d* word—ever. Banish it from your vocabulary and banish its effects from your whole life.

So far this ritual has worked wonders. If my girlfriend and I are doing anything, we are "seeing" people. The word "seeing" is far more positive and carries little or no baggage. The best story she told me was that not long after doing this, a guy asked her for a "d—" and she said to him, "I am not seeing other people right now—I am seeing myself."

And she really was—all that energy she had been putting out there trying to "D#*!" men, she instead turned toward herself. And like a truly successful Bewitcher, she bewitched herself and then aimed her attention outward and now happily has a boyfriend—yes, a real proper boyfriend who doesn't shy away from commitment and is a really nice bloke!

> The "burying" aspect of this spell is very adaptable for any number of unpleasant things you want to banish from your life. As before, just write it on a piece of paper, cross with garlic, "blow away," and then dig a hole, place the stone on top, and cover with earth. If you want to undo the spell, just dig up the paper. Presto, it is done!

"THOU SHALT LOVE THYSELF— NO MATTER WHAT!" RITUAL

There is no excuse not to love yourself—there really isn't. If there is one thing you can absolutely rely on in life, it is that you will be there for it.

But sometimes it is so hard not to feel trashed and

Bewitch a Man

overwhelmed by how no one else will love you. Especially when you have worked hard on doing your positive affirmations, writing nice things to yourself, spoiling yourself with a spa day and all that good stuff, and still you feel worn out and empty and down.

This spell will absolutely fix your self-esteem. It is very powerful and involves a drop of blood, but please don't freak out. Blood is the elixir of life, and you only need a little of it for this spell.

You will need these items:
- Blooming flowering plant, preferably with red or pink blossoms (roses and orchids are great)
- One sharp pin
- Neosporin or other antibacterial ointment to put on your finger after you've jabbed it with a pin
- Rose quartz crystals or even pink glass pebbles (though the crystals are better)

You must perform this bewitchery naked and perfect—sky clad, in other words. Stand in front of the mirror and blow a kiss to yourself three times, and then smile and simply say these words:

I love you—I really do.

Prick your finger with the pin and let some drops of your blood anoint the flowers of the plant. Pop some ointment onto your finger if you like, and a Band-Aid, too, if you really jabbed yourself. Now stud the earth around the flowering plant with the crystals. Say the following incantation:

Love's blood blossoms
and flows in my veins.
Ecstasy fills me sweetly.
All I need is inside me.

Water and nurture the plant. Every morning take a crystal from the base of the plant and carry it with you—swapping out for another one the next day. Now you are plugged into your own source of unconditional love.

And love attracts love.

Bewitch a Man

Chapter Seven

Sexy Hexy

THE BENEFITS OF SEX MAGICK IN BEWITCHING A man cannot be underestimated—and I don't mean the obvious stuff of being a great lay in the sack, or dressing provocatively or flirting outrageously at a bar. The power of orgasm, sexual elixirs like semen and your own sexual juices, and the act of sex itself are potent tools to be used for transformation, elevation, and control in all areas of love and passion. Bewitchers understand nature to be sacred, and thus our physical bodies—our direct link to the natural world—are considered divine. Fertility is honored as holy, and the act of lovemaking is a recognized part of the procreative universal consciousness that unites all beings. In this section I have included some of the most powerful sex magick spells, tricks, and disciplines that you can add to your bewitchery arsenal.

The bottom line is that men are pretty simple—nature made them that way. They are sexual creatures first and foremost—all the other layers of their persona come after that. That is why you need to initially bewitch them with an alluring sexual presence.

Again, remember to approach sex magick with a sense of reverence and awe at the magnificence of your body and your ability to love and lust. Know that as you explore the magickal power of the orgasm and your sacred sensuality, you are diving into the ocean of pure joy that is at the core of all creation.

BEWITCHERS' ULTIMATE LOVE SPELL

This is one of the most powerful love spells known, utterly ancient in its origins and very effective. There is literally no limit to the positive results of this love spell. It uses the most sacred and extraordinary of all power sources—the human orgasm. And it is so very simple.

Lie in bed alone at night and picture the one that you desire. Say his name over and over in your head as

Bewitch a Man

you pleasure yourself—and as you approach the peak of orgasm, start saying his name out loud. If there is not a particular person that you want to bewitch, then say "love and bliss" over and over because that is at heart what you want to conjure into your life.

As your orgasm subsides and your body is still rushing with pleasurable feelings, seal the spell by saying the following:

> *I offer my sacred pleasure to the universe.*
> *May it magnify the joy at the core of all creation*
> *so that all may flourish in peace and harmony.*

Yes, it's a bit of a formal mouthful but worth memorizing, as it really honors your sex magick as a divine act. I promise that you are doing something very sacred and holy when you celebrate the divine gift of orgasm. In fact, it's like saying a prayer—only it's a lot more fun!

ENHANCE YOUR ORGASM SPELL WITH YOUR SACRED-RITUAL TOOLS

Bewitchers from ages past knew the power of using sacred-ritual tools consecrated to work in alignment with their magickal goals. In this modern age, it is important that you gather your ritual tools with reverence and diligence. I will give you a tip on how best to procure these essential accoutrements of your bewitching craft.

Walk into a sex shop or jump on the Internet and place an order.

Oh, I know—you were expecting me to say that you were going to have to book a ticket to Romania to find an ancient magick wand with your name carved in it. Not so. Ritual tools more often than not really only carry the power that you convey onto them—and when you use sex toys for the very potent weaving of sex magick, they are going to carry a lot of that transformational energy.

Fittingly enough, my most personally empowered ritual sex-toy tool is called "The Magic Wand"! It is actually a back and neck massager, but when it's between my legs, it produces a particularly lovely and magickal result! The orgasms I can conjure using this sacred tool are very potent, and I can direct them with great force and intent toward my intended goal— whether that be to find new love, enhance a new love, or even send unwanted love away. It all depends on what I am thinking as I orgasm.

Unlike a lot of other books on sex and love magick

Bewitch a Man

you may have read, I am not suggesting you go out and try to procure exotic herbs and statues of ancient phallic and vulval totems. No way. Just go out and procure a vast selection of exotic, ritual sex toys for your personal pleasure!

Color is a great ally in bewitchery. Different colors endow meaning and consist of vibrational energy that can affect emotions and enhance magickal manifestation. You can use color magick in many ways, from what color lingerie to wear to what color paper to wrap a gift in to what color your sex toys should be!

Here is a special chart to help guide you in your choices:
- PINK = romantic love
- RED = unbridled passion
- BLUE = patience and persistence
- BLACK = mystery
- GREEN = money
- WHITE = purity and protection, aligned with virginlike innocence

- YELLOW = creative and intellectual challenge (think Twister sex positions and intelligent conversation after sex)
- GOLD = bewitches him with your desire
- SILVER = increases your self-appreciation
- NUDE = no masks, life-partner commitment

SPELL TO HEAL A LOW LIBIDO (ONE FOR YOU AND ONE FOR HIM)

Imagine this . . . you have busted your butt to bewitch a guy, and he is in your bedroom and totally keen—but you are just not feeling that horny and you didn't feel horny last time you were in bed together either. Mentally you want to . . . but you are just not able. Maybe it's nerves, maybe you're bored with him already . . . but you want to follow through with the physical act. This spell can help. Do it a few nights in a row before you see him, or if caught short, you can even do it on the night you *are* seeing him. But it does increase in power if you can do it a few nights in a row and as a regular discipline. It will definitely keep your libido peaking.

You will need these items:
- Red candle (for lust)

Bewitch a Man

- Lavender oil (for pure intent and love)
- Warm honey (blessed by bees, ancient symbol of the goddess of fertility)

Take the red candle and warm the wax by dipping it in boiling water. Carve seven notches down one side about one-quarter inch apart. Massage lavender oil sensuously into the candle and then light it. Gaze into the flame, place a drop of honey on your tongue, and say these words:

By sacred oil and lusty fire
honey sweet is my desire.

Gaze into the flame, concentrating on feeling a warm rush of passion move through you. Visualize that sweet honey flowing into your core. As the candlelight falls on your body, imagine your lover caressing you in a warm, sensuous embrace that awakens your passion. Continue to visualize this until the candle has burned down one notch.

Snuff the flame and do this ritual every night as often as you need to. If you start this ritual on a Friday, a day that is blessed by Venus, the planet of love, and continue until the following Friday, the effects of the spell should last a good full-moon span (i.e., four weeks) or even longer.

The spell to improve a *guy's* libido is simple but very effective if done with sincere intent. I created this spell for a girlfriend who had been with her guy for a while and loved him, but he was letting work and stress into the bedroom, and their sex life was floundering. I advised her to do the following spell every day for a week, from Friday to Friday, and then let the results manifest. She didn't even need to wait till the following Friday. By the weekend, they were having great sex.

You will need these items:
- Red candle
- Cinnamon paste—made by mixing half a teaspoon of cinnamon powder in one teaspoon of olive oil (cinnamon is a potent male aphrodisiac)

Hold the candle in your left hand, and smear some of the paste on the candle as you close your eyes and firmly state the following three times:

I name thee [his name].
This spell is invoked to increase your passion
so that you can fulfill me with wild abandon.

Burn the candle in the bedroom before he arrives, to start creating an environment of lusty energy. Trust and believe your spell will work and watch him rise to the occasion!

SACRED SEX PICNIC AT HOME

This is a great, fun, seductive event, particularly perfect with a brand-new partner to get you off to a great start together, but also wonderful at any stage of your relationship. And of course, if you are in a monogamous relationship (and using other birth control), you may choose to leave out the condoms!

You will need these items:
- Pink strawberry-flavored condoms (for love and fun)
- Massage oil that features some or all of the following essential oils—ylang-ylang, rose, geranium, patchouli, sandalwood, vanilla, and coconut (all pure aphrodisiacs)
- Musk and patchouli incense (for lust)
- Red and pink candles (for love and passion)
- Pink tiger-lily flowers or other opulent, pink, sweetly scented blooms

- Vanilla-bean ice cream (for happiness)
- White, soft feathers
- Nice big rug—if you want to be traditional, maybe use a checkered picnic blanket, or to make it super-sensual, use a lovely fake-fur throw

Set up your space with candles and incense burning. Place the flowers in vases and scatter the feathers around so the area is opulent and inviting.

Honor the God within your lover by indulging him in sensual pleasures—tickle him with feathers, eat ice cream off his chest, massage the warm oil into his skin, maybe even drip some of the candle wax on him for extra excitement—and have fun using the condoms! Approach the whole sacred sex picnic as an act of worship. The more you revel in the pleasure that is our divine right as humans, the more bewitched your man will be, and the positive energy that you generate will flow into all areas of your life.

Bewitch a Man

LOVEMAKING CONFIDENCE TIPS

If you are diligently practicing all your bewitching techniques, but you still feel a bit nervous being naked in front of your newly bewitched guy, here are some magickal tips:

The powerful, passionate element of fire that can transform and liberate is contained in the wonders of candlelight! Lots of red and pink candles will encourage passion. Burn some ylang-ylang essential oil in an essential-oil burner for sensuality and confidence, and repeat this mantra in your head at least twenty times:

I choose to be here, I am in control.
My body is divine. . . .
He is a lucky bastard to be in my presence!

THE "I GUARANTEE THIS WON'T BE A ONE-NIGHT STAND" SPELLS

Here are a few relatively benign and sweet little rituals you can perform to ensure that your first visit to his bed won't be the last.

No. 1: Tie a love charm under his bed. Love charms are easy to make. Get a fresh, scented red rose and hang it upside down to dry, and when it is dry, trim the stem to about an inch long and tie some of your hair to it (or if you really don't want to potentially wreck the masterpiece your hairdresser crowned you with, wear a simple silver chain around your left wrist for one week, and then wrap this around the dried rose, securing it well).

Kiss the rose three times. For extra potency, you can lick it if you want (as you do this, think about how you want to devour him when he is yours) and then put the lot in a discreet, black cloth drawstring bag. Tie this to one of the legs of his bed—or if that is too obvious, tuck it in among the junk he keeps under his bed, or place it right in the middle of his mattress on the box spring. But it works best discreetly tied to the bed leg so the energies can circulate.

No. 2: If you haven't had time to prepare a love charm and want to do something more spontaneous, tuck a few strands of your hair or your undies under his mattress. If you are worried undies will be too easily discovered under his mattress, you can always throw them into the back of his closet or tuck them inside a pair of socks he is unlikely to wear, at the rear of his underwear drawer. Get creative and be sneaky (in the most positive and harmonious way, of course)! Your little love charm must not be seen with his naked eye, or its effect will be erased.

No. 3: Kiss his mirror where he won't see it but where his face or body will be reflected. This way, your affection for him will be bounced back to him every time he looks at himself. A good place to do this is at the bathroom vanity, but not at eye level; perhaps at tap level, which is most likely in line with his groin—always a nice place to focus your affections!

THE MOREGASMIC MASSAGE

Simple and sweet—one of the nicest ways to endear yourself to a man is to give a great neck rub. Add magick to the equation with the powers of visualization and conscious color-energy channeling, and you are working bewitchery!

Give a great neck rub, but as you do this, visualize hot red energy flowing from your fingertips straight to his phallus. Don't laugh—just try it. Breathe deep, long, and slow, and in your mind's eye, as you are rubbing his neck, see your hands caressing his manhood. Remember, red is the color of unbridled passion and lust, so keep seeing that color rushing into him from your hands.

If you are more keen to make him fall sweetly and coyly in love with you, see pink light. If it is someone you have been dating awhile and you have had problems with communication, see a cool blue light flood into his body. Finish every neck rub with a gentle kiss behind his ear to confer your power over him and your bewitching presence in his mind. He will not be able to stop thinking about you and dreaming of having your hands upon him again.

ADVANCED BEWITCHING TECHNIQUE: SLEEPING WITH A GUY JUST FOR SEX

This is a tough one and must be practiced by only extremely advanced Bewitchers possessing great bewitchery discipline. The situation: If, with all your advanced Bewitcher powers, you know that a guy is in no way relationship material, yet you still want to have sex with him, you can do so, but YOU MUST WALK AWAY after it. Shag him somewhere where you can get out of bed (or out of the car, the bathroom in the nightclub, or wherever) and go home STRAIGHT AWAY. Don't hang around and fall asleep in his arms or let him drive you home or any other potentially emotionally confusing thing like that.

And always have safe sex. Use a black condom so that it binds you from falling under the spell of his magical cock (the color black binds and banishes). Do not fall in love. If by accident you do fall in love, do the "I'm Not in Love" spell on page 182.

Chapter Eight

TOOLS OF THE TRADE

WORKING WITH CANDLES IS ONE OF THE SIMPLEST and most rewarding types of bewitchery. When lit, candles invoke the element of fire—the most dynamic of the four sacred natural elements (the other three being air, earth, and water). Fire works fast to bring positive change. All the following spells can rev up your love life rapidly.

LOVE CANDLES

I teach spell crafting and magick workshops at the Learning Annex, but I rarely have time to take any of their courses myself. Luckily, I was able to sneak into one of their "Candle Making" workshops. Everyone else was making candles that would smell nice in their bathrooms—I was doing bewitchery!

The good news is that making candles is super easy, and for bewitchery, it's so much more effective to do your own, ones that you can enchant from the get-go so that they are super-empowered with your intent.

You will need the following per candle:

- Half cup of green apple peel (not the juicy pulp), grated
- Two teaspoons of dried basil
- One cup of wax (pink for new love or red for charging up existing love), preferably vegetable or soy wax. (You can break up existing candles to melt and remold if you can't find the raw wax.)
- Rose quartz crystal about the size of a small pebble
- Essential oils blessed for love, such as vanilla, cinnamon, rose, ylang-ylang, violet, or neroli
- Heat-resistant container (milk carton or greased flower pot, to be used as a candle mold, or a glass in which the wax can stay)

- A stick long enough to span the opening of the container
- Wick long enough to hang from the stick to the bottom of the container

Using a double-boiler saucepan, warm the cup of wax and carefully stir in the grated apple, essential oil, and basil. While the wax is melting, get your container ready. Tie the wick to the center of the stick, making sure that the stick will be level when balanced across the top of the container. The wick must always touch the bottom of the container, and to ensure this and give your enchanted love candle extra oomph, tie it around a piece of rose quartz crystal. Kiss the crystal three times and ask for it to bless your love life every time the flame is lit.

Once you've poured the hot wax into the container and the wax has hardened, remove the candle from the mold and cut the wick to the appropriate length, or if you are leaving the candle in a glass, just cut the wick.

Now comes the fun, creative stuff. Check the following list of bewitching symbols, and using a pin or pointed knife, carve your chosen symbols of love into the candle:

- Heart = magnifies love
- Key = opens all doors to love
- Chain = links lives together
- Horseshoe = promises luck in all matters of love
- Bell = encourages a proposal or blesses an anniversary
- Coin = encourages wealth of spirit and love
- Flower = magnifies personal beauty

After carving your symbol, carve your initials and the initials of the person you wish to bewitch or are in the process of bewitching. You can carve into the side of the candle, or on the top if you are leaving it in a glass container.

You now have a love-enchanted candle that when lit will bring true love to you or make your current love passionate and thrilling.

A SIMPLE METHOD OF ENCHANTED-CANDLE BURNING

Note: Please know that burning enchanted candles for bewitchery is not like lighting tea lights and votive candles to illuminate the dinner table. Lighting enchanted candles is an act of bewitchery, and your

Bewitch a Man

magickal efforts are worthy of respect—mostly your own respect, so take your efforts seriously and follow this guide.

candle burning times

Burn your candle on the full moon to encourage companionship. Let it burn for two hours if you desire to be a happy couple. If you are into three-somes, burn the candle for three hours. Basically add an hour for every desired partner!

On a Friday, burn the candle at noon for one hour and then again at six p.m. for one hour. Why Friday? Ruled by Venus, blessed with love and passion, Friday is a great day to burn love candles. Also, it's the first evening of the weekend, and lots of other people will be thinking about good times and romantic adventures. You can tap into that energy and magnify it into your life, allowing your love and bewitching dreams to come true.

A DEVIOUS CANDLELIGHT TRICK THAT WORKS

If the light of an enchanted candle falls on the face of your desired one—he will be yours. It has to be the light of the candle, though, and not electric light.

Here is a good ploy you can use. Invite your chosen one over and say that there is a power outage. Have your enchanted candles lit around the house—and hold one up to his face as he enters. As the light falls on his face, in your mind repeat to yourself three times, *Be mine. Be mine. Be mine.* He will be.

DON'T BLOW AWAY THE MAGICK

You should always snuff the candles so that you do not blow away the spell you are casting. If you are going to extinguish a flame, make a statement of intent like the following:

I blow away anything that prevents me from being happy and fulfilled.

If you cannot effectively snuff them, you can "kiss" out your love candles (blow kisses at them). Whenever I have to blow out any candles, I say the following enchantment:

I blow away all obstacles that prevent me from achieving my greatest good and highest goals.

Here are ways to enchant your lovemaking space so that it always makes you happy and satisfied.

YOUR BEDROOM

Always keep a single white flower, like a fragrant gardenia or rose, next to your bed. This will bless any activity there with purity of intent.

Throw a pinch of sea salt under your bed before company arrives, and your bed will be a sacred space for love that will enhance and not break your heart.

Spicy, warm-scented candles of cocoa, cinnamon, or vanilla, or earthy scents like cedar and pine, will make a man feel more welcome in your bedroom than floral scents.

love-bed charm

Tie this love charm to the leg of your bed on the side where he will sleep, and he will stay entranced with you.

You will need these items:

- Photo of him (if you don't have a photo,

draw a picture of him as best you can and write his initials on it)

- Lock of your hair
- Plant vine of some sort (ivy is perfect, but anything that can be wrapped and tied off is fine)
- Red cloth bag (you can also use a red paper envelope)

Kiss the photo of him three times.

Place the photo in the red bag with the lock of your hair, and close the bag.

Bind the bag to the leg of the bed with the vine, wrapping around the leg at least three times to firmly secure the bag. Repeat this mantra as you do it:

Your love is mine for all time.

When you want to break it off with him, simply remove the charm and throw it away. He will not return to your bed.

"I was a little obsessed with watching Charmed at the time. I think it was my first real introduction to fun, girly witchcraft. Anyway, I worked above a New Age bookstore and was passing some time there one afternoon when I noticed Fiona's book and started *flipping the pages. I was inspired by the fun writing style and excited to do some spells, so off I went with my book in my brown paper bag, feeling like I was about to embark on a secret-society mission.*

I was dating a man I shouldn't have been dating (we worked together and he was also a bit of a ladies' man). We were both seeing other people, but I really liked him and wanted to see him exclusively so I did the 'how to make someone fall in love with you' spell. I did the spell, and then two days later he told me he loved me. Even funnier, he kept saying, 'I feel like you have cast a spell on me.' I was totally freaked out and told my girlfriends. One of them stole my book and I never did get it back!"

—JUSTINE, NEW YORK

HIS BEDROOM

Always tuck a pair of your undies (worn) beneath his mattress to keep your place secure there. Retrieve them when you are no longer interested in being with him. If you can't retrieve them—buy one new pair with the intention of "owning" them again, and it will effectively end the magick you did by putting the original pair under his mattress.

Give him a gift that he will keep in his bedroom—something that you know is cool and that he will like but that is not obviously romantic. Some ideas are a coin tray (aligned with abundance of interest in you), a small subtle art piece made from wood (aligned with strength of intention and male energies), or a pen-notepad set for jotting down, before he falls asleep, things to do the next day (like take you out to dinner).

Before you give your gift to him, you are going to enchant it so that it carries your energy and keeps him bewitched. Hold the gift to your heart, close your eyes, and imagine him clearly in your mind. Take three deep breaths, and as you breathe out, see your breath as your will flowing through the gift. Then open your eyes, lick the tip of your right index finger and trace an X (like a kiss) on the bottom of the gift in your spit, and say the following:

Your love is mine, for all time.

Give him the gift in a casual, friendly way when you are going to bed one night. As long as your gift is not traditionally romantic, but more functional in design and aligned with his interests, he will happily accept it and not pick up any vibes that you are bewitching him intentionally. He will only think that you are a dear, sweet, and incredibly cool person—and continue to fall in love with you, never suspecting that in his room there is now a homing signal that draws your presence back there repeatedly!

When you no longer want him in your life, it would be a good idea to retrieve the gift. But if you can't manage that, you can erase the gift enchantment by simply closing your eyes, picturing it in your mind, clapping your hands loudly three times, and seeing it "disappear." Say these words out loud:

I declare the magick over
As is my will, so must it be
For the good of all, but mostly for me

BEWITCHING LOVE AMULETS

Happily, charm bracelets and necklaces are entrenched back in the fashion world, and your bewitchery will draw no curious looks—only admiring ones.

You can also sew charms into clothes (yours or your bewitched man's), carry them in your pocket, bury them by your front door, or whatever else you feel is appropriate as you bewitch your world.

Find the charms on the Internet if you haven't got time to shop in the real world. Please note that often the best places to find gorgeous charms are at flea markets, garage sales, and country fairs.

You can also make your own charmed jewelry and be creative in how you string pieces together. Use black velvet for seriousness of intent, pink ribbon to magnify the light of love, or choose a heavy silver chain to link your energy to him. Wear one or a selection of symbols from page 135, as your intent and needs require.

Chapter Nine

Apples and Potions: The Stuff of Fairy Tales

APPLES HAVE BEEN USED SINCE TIME IMMEMORIAL TO conjure, bless, magnify, and sweeten love. They are the most enchanted fruit on the planet! The following are bewitching uses for apples. A trip to the grocer will never be the same again as you bewitch your love life with apples!

1. To know the initials of your soul mate use two red apples with the stems intact. (Use organic for extra blessings of Goddess Earth!) At midnight

on a full moon, kiss both apples, and say, *Reveal to me my beloved's identity.*

Then slowly twist the stem of one apple while saying the letters of the alphabet. The letter you speak when the stem breaks off is your beloved's first initial. Do the same with the second apple to find the initial of his last name. Be on the lookout for any person you meet with these initials.

2. In ancient times it was traditional to eat an apple together on the wedding night. Go with your lover to an orchard and pick apples together. Cut the first one you pick, and feed three slices to him while gazing into his eyes. He will be yours forever.

3. Norse myth said that to encourage potency in your man, you drop an apple into his lap. I don't know if I would recommend this, as you may damage the crown jewels! But a friend of mine got married and wanted a baby, so I had a pair of boxer shorts made from material with an apple print on them for her to give to her husband. She was pregnant within two months!

4. Do like the ancient Greeks and throw an apple at your desired one to make them burn with lust. WARNING: I tried this once when I was a bit tipsy

and hit the guy in the head—not good! A modern variation is to cut some slices of apple and throw them in the path of your desired one. When he steps on them, he will be alive with passion for you.

5. "The apple of my eye" is a common saying that is a sign of great affection. To invoke this energy, place apples over your eyes instead of cucumbers. (As we know, cucumbers are a fantastic way to reduce puffiness and brighten eyes. Apples work in a similar way. Use green apples for their slightly astringent qualities.)

6. In the Garden of Eden the serpent lived in an apple tree. In pre-Christian spirituality the serpent was a very sacred and beautiful symbol of the Goddess and her great wisdom and eternally regenerative life forces. To invoke the blessings of wisdom and make the right choices in love, eat an apple before going out with your girlfriends to meet men. The added bonus is that a healthy treat like this will give you the energy to dance the night away!

7. There is a Jewish folktale called "The Magic Apple." The story says that to perform a good mitzvah (a worthy deed), you must give up something you have. Celebrate and align yourself with

this sweet tale by giving a basket of apples that you have picked and polished by hand to someone that you have a crush on. (As an offering to the universe to ensure the man returns your love, plant an apple tree to continue the magick.)

8. A fun Halloween tradition is bobbing for apples. Be like the maidens of old Scotland, and after successfully bobbing, partially peel the apple you capture, pass the peel counterclockwise around your head three times, and toss it over your shoulder. When it lands, the skin will form the first letter of your true love's name.

9. When you rub an apple against your shirt to polish it, you are actually continuing an ancient ritual. Ancient Celts did it to drive out evil nature spirits and fairies, and medieval Christians thought doing this would protect them from the Devil's grasp. Rub an apple on your shirt over your heart a few times with your eyes closed and see the action driving away loneliness. Then open your eyes and take a big bite to represent how you are ready to gorge yourself on love and adoration from your bewitched man.

10. Remember how Eve tempted Adam in the Garden of Eden with an apple? Well, apples are considered

Bewitch a Man

to have great seductive powers. If you want a man to be transfixed by you, cut an apple into slivers, dip them in a little sugar and honey (to further sweeten love), and feed them to him by hand . . . wearing a fabulous lacy pair of undies and a bra that you just bought to seal the deal.

LOVE POTIONS

Mixing up a magickal love potion is the art of alchemy— transforming raw ingredients into a substance greater and more valuable than the sum of its parts. As you extract, blend, and stir these potent concoctions, you are not only making great-tasting libations but also whipping your love intentions into a powerful medium capable of transporting them straight into the person you are aiming for!

SEXY LOVE POTION

This is my favorite love potion. It tastes divinely seductive and has great aphrodisiacal powers. Remember, magick works because of the intent with which you fuel it, and all acts of love and pleasure are sacred to the Goddess. This potion will definitely have your man acting in a divine manner!

Get these ingredients:
- Damiana (a sacred herb of seduction from exotic South America)
- High-quality vodka (like Grey Goose or Belvedere)
- French champagne (sacred to the goddess of passion, Aphrodite)
- Strawberry juice (blessed with love)
- Honey (sweetens desire)

Soak a large handful of dried damiana leaves in sixteen ounces (five hundred milliliters) of vodka for five days.

Then strain through a conical filter paper into a bowl. Discard the herbs.

Slowly stir in a half cup of excellent-quality honey in a sunwise direction to invoke positive power.

Now is the time to work love magick with the following act of alchemy. Visualize you and the man of your desire making love with wild abandon and chant these words:

Aphrodite, hear my plea.
[His name] madly desires me.
So must it be, so must it be.

Bewitch a Man

When the honey is dissolved, set the vodka infusion in the fridge. On the special night have lots of scented candles (vanilla, chocolate, and cinnamon scented will be perfect) and make your magick.

In a shaker glass with ice, mix two ounces of the infused vodka with one ounce of champagne and a splash of strawberry juice.

As you pour your love potion into a large martini glass, again state your magickal, sexy love chant. Serve with a dish of lush dark-chocolate treats (chocolate is another supersexy aphrodisiac) and have a passionate evening!

QUICK AND EASY LOVE POTIONS

These are very simple to make but feature powerful ingredients aligned with enhancing love and passion. Remember, magick works because the intent with which you fuel it, so as you mix and serve these drinks, visualize what you want—basically, him to be madly and passionately in love with you!

CHAMPAGNE LOVE SHOTS

Simple and sweet, this concoction will awaken ebullience and passion in both of you.

Get these ingredients:
- Good champagne
- Two tablespoons of a single-fruit puree (choose from raspberry, passion fruit, peach, or pomegranate, which are all sacred to love and seduction)

Spoon the puree into a champagne flute, and slowly pour the champagne on top as you visualize in your mind the two of you laughing and flirting.

LUSTY MARTINI

This is laced with intoxicatingly lovely aphrodisiacal ingredients! Don't let him drink so many of these that he can't be attentive to you in the sack, though!

Get these ingredients:
- Two ounces Stolichnaya vanilla vodka
- One ounce Godiva liqueur
- Splash of orange curaçao

Shake ingredients and serve with a chocolate-dipped strawberry on the side. Feed the strawberry to him while visualizing both of you staying in bed and making love for the whole weekend!

Bewitch a Man

NECTAR OF THE LOVE GODS

Rosé is a sexy pink wine that is perfect to serve for all scenes of seduction. Pink is the color of love, and wine is sacred to the gods. Sip a little and pour some of it as a libation onto the earth when you are standing next to your man, and the gods will bless your union with passion. Just don't let him see you tipping it out or he may think you are a bit cuckoo!

NONALCOHOLIC PASSION POTION

It is not necessary to use alcohol when making love potions. The following potion is very good for sipping over ice, in between long, lingering kisses! It is also particularly good to serve when someone who has genuine feelings for you cannot seem to get past his nervousness. It will encourage his passion to take priority over his fear and nerves.

You will need these ingredients:
- Orange juice (for energy and light)
- Cranberry juice (for sincerity)
- Strawberry juice (for love and passion)
- Sugar (for sweetness)
- Half a lemon (for purity of intent)

In a pitcher, combine equal quantities each of the juices.

Stir the potion sunwise with a spoon; feel your desire for him course through you, and channel it into the potion as you chant this passion-inducing invocation:

Fruits of love and passion afire.
Make him burn with desire.

Before serving, trace around the rim of a tall glass with the lemon, and then dip the glass into the bowl of sugar before filling. If this drink seems overly sweet to you, you can skip dipping the glass in sugar and you can also dilute the juice by filling the glass three-fourths full and then topping with sparkling mineral water. It will still have a potent magickal effect if you focus hard when you stir the passion in.

SHARE THE LOVE

When enjoying your love potions, always pour a little on the earth as a libation to the Goddess to say thank you for this divine opportunity to work your magick and bewitch your man.

Bewitch a Man

Chapter Ten

IT'S A BEWITCHING WORLD

INSPIRE AWE IN OTHERS AND YOURSELF AS YOU align yourself with the elements of nature. The regenerative abundance of the natural world is something you can harness for your own personal energy source. Pure and potent nature rituals can capture the beauty of flowers, the strength of mountains, the nobility of trees, the sensuousness of the ocean, the radiance of the sun, and the mystery of the moon. Nature rituals are incredibly nurturing in a practical way and also work magickally to transform you at the very core of your being and make you even more magnificent and marvelous to the man you are bewitching.

Every time you speak, breath flows over your lips—a sweet torrent of the sacred element of air, which can be put to magickal use by forming words that bless and empower you when you bewitch the moment.

You can bless and empower an important relationship in your life, whether that be with yourself or a partner, new or long term. The way to do this is to have a bewitching word of the day. Only you can know the word (which is chosen in the morning by you). It may be the word "ecstatic" or "appreciate" or "beautiful" or "goddess" or "happy." *Any* word you choose that day.

When anyone says the bewitching word or you read it or even see it on a billboard, you must drop what you are doing, take a deep breath, and exhale the word on your breath. Then take a few moments' time-out for love and affection—for either yourself or your partner. So, you might be stuck in traffic on a freeway and see it on a billboard, and instead of sitting there cursing and giving other drivers filthy looks, you will give yourself a hug and say out loud that you love and appreciate yourself. Or you may hear it on the evening news and reach over and kiss your partner's neck and give him a little neck rub. However you want to express love and affection spontaneously will be perfect and blessed by the transformational energies of air lifting the wings of your sacred word.

HARNESS THE STRENGTH OF MOUNTAINS

Make the earth move for you every day by capturing it and carrying it with you. Go somewhere beautiful that inspires you. Maybe it is the top of the canyon you hike to every weekend or a cliff top over the ocean. It needs to be a place that, once you are there, you feel free and on top of the world. Sunrise is a lovely time to do this ritual, as it will be a private and peaceful time when you can get really connected with the earth energy.

Take a little empty box with you and an orange ribbon or tie. Wear something clean and noble in appearance. Even just a simple white T-shirt worn with intent will say that you are ready to receive the blessings of the mountain as an honor. If you have to sweat and climb to get to the top of the mountain, take a clean T-shirt with you to put on before you do the ritual.

Let your intuition guide you to a place where you can sit directly on the earth and pick up some of the dirt in front of you and rub it through your fingers.

Concentrate on its texture and earthy, reassuring smell. This is the stuff of mountains—bold and powerful. Now sit or stand very upright and strong, and consciously connect with the great ancient strength of the earth upon which you perch. Take long slow breaths and draw in that energy, seeing it spiral up through your spine and into the bones of your body. Know you now resonate with the strength of a mountain, and that empowers you every step of the way. Know that you carry that fortitude within you, reserved for whenever you need it during the trials and challenges of your life—especially your love life.

Place a hand to the earth and say the following:

I am blessed by your strength.

Pick up some of the earth and place it in your box. Tie the orange ribbon around it, and say these words:

It is done—I carry the strength of the mountain in my heart.

Leave an offering for the mountain. Maybe you can bury a strand of your hair in the dirt that you loosened with your hand, or if you are carrying a water bottle and food, pour a little water and crumble a little food upon the earth. Do this mountain ritual regularly, and you will project a calm, confident energy that will appeal to men looking for a companion and long-term partner.

THE FLOWERS OF ROMANCE

Surround yourself with flowers. Put vases of them around your home, and turn your whole living space into a temple of tantric temptation. You can even bring love and positive vibes into a challenging work space with flowers. Your office mates will love you for it, and too much love is not enough!

Here are some other ways to bring more romance into your life using the power of flowers:

1. Float flowers in the bath, in bowls, or in any sink—even the kitchen sink! Flowers floating in water honor the Hindu thousand-petal Lotus of Enlightenment that floats in the nectar of knowledge and will bless your space with love and wisdom.

2. Decorate a main meal as well as the dessert with edible flowers.

3. Cover yourself with petals and nothing else and call out to your lover.

4. Scatter petals across your front doorstep so that all who enter are blessed. (You can even do this at your office so that only people who will be nice to you will enter your space.)

5. Tie flowers to ribbon when wrapping a gift and it will bind your love to the present.

6. Put flowers in your bewitched man's pockets or briefcase as a clue that there are special plans for that evening.

7. Wear flowers in your hair. Try a few bound into a sleek chignon, or if you have short hair, around your neck wear a choker with a fresh rose or gardenia stitched to it. And wear the flower with intent, not just because it is beautiful—but because YOU are. Men will respond to your awakened self-appreciation.

8. For birthday fun (or indeed anytime!), place dry petals in a balloon (stretch the opening with tongs). Then tell the person to make a wish and pop the balloon over his or her head to make it come true. They will be showered with petals bestowing abundance of good fortune.

9. Conjure more love in your life by writing the

name of your bewitched in petals and gently blowing your breath across them three times, knowing as you do this, you are breathing life into your love.

10. Toss a handful of dried rose petals onto an open fire, and fan the smoke to the sky with your hands to call on love (like mating-call smoke signals!).

Remember: The more love, smiles, and flowers you give, the more you shall receive!

LOVE-LOLLIPOP MAGICK

Make a sweet treat even sweeter by adding enchanted flowers.

You will need these items:
- Your favorite hard candy in colors of red and pink (the equivalent of approximately sixteen tablespoons when finely crushed)
- Eight cookie cutters in the shape of hearts
- Slivers of rose petals and/or finely trimmed
- lavender buds
- Baking tray
- Foil
- Lollipop sticks

When you trim the petals or lavender buds, blow a kiss to them and say this charm to enchant them:

Flowers blessed with a kiss
bestow love on those who lick
the sacred sweet delicious heart
of which you now become a part.

Place your candy in a heavy plastic bag and place on top of a wooden chopping block (or folded towel). Crush them with a meat mallet or hammer.

You will need two tablespoons of crushed candy per cookie cutter. I suggest using heart-shaped cookie cutters because the shape of a heart is aligned with love magick (obviously!).

Line a baking tray with foil and put cookie cutters on it at least two inches apart. Place a candy layer in each cutter about one-quarter to one-half inch thick. Now sprinkle into the cookie cutters one teaspoon of rose petal or lavender pieces, cut up small. Blow little kisses to each Love Lollipop again, further blessing them with love-attraction energy.

Finally, scatter one half tablespoon of crushed candy on top of the petals.

Bewitch a Man

Place the tray in a 350 degree F oven for six to eight minutes or until candies are completely melted. Take them out and let them cool for thirty seconds. Remove the cookie cutters carefully with tongs. The melted candy will spread slightly when you do this. Quickly attach a stick to the base of each Love Lollipop, twisting the stick to cover its end with melted candy. While the candy is still hot, you can gently press some more flower petals into the surface with a fork, if you like. Let cool completely and peel foil from the Love Lollipops.

You can serve Love Lollipops to your fellow Bewitchers to enhance their love lives, or give one to the man you are bewitching—or just enjoy them all yourself!

OCEAN MAGICK

All life came from the ocean, and its shifting tides represent the ebb and flow of love in our lives. Spend as much time as you can by the sea. I am a professional scuba diver and when I commune with the natural world underwater, everything makes sense. I am filled with so much love and appreciation for our beautiful planet and the extraordinary privilege it is to be alive that any love drama that may be around me fades away to insignificance. Alternatively, if I am in a budding relationship or in the process of bewitching a man, scuba diving enhances my self-appreciation and makes me feel empowered, and this only makes me more impressive and appealing to the man I have my sights set on!

OCEAN WATER WISH FOR BLISS

This little bewitchery is so simple but very effective. Take a glass bottle to the ocean and get about a cup of seawater. Blow three kisses to the sea to thank her for sharing her blessings with you. Now go to the home of the man you adore, and pour the seawater over his doorstep before stepping across it into his home. You have just blessed your relationship with him with abundant love and good energy.

SACRED TREES

As humans have evolved, we have forged a unique relationship with trees—they provide so many things for us, from shelter and food to fuel and inspiration. Interacting with the magick of trees is a powerful activity for a Bewitcher in any context and especially when bewitching a man.

When I was working on a television show a couple of years ago, I had a remarkable experience. I would start my day on location with a long walk through a beautiful old garden, and on one particular morning I had a conversation with God. And when I say "God," I mean a male deity presence. In fact, I felt I was speaking with a Christian interpretation of God—a fatherlike figure.

I sat quietly as I contemplated the many beautiful old trees around me, and a hawk flew over and perched only a few feet away from me. "Look at the trees in the garden," I heard a male voice say. It seemed to be coming from the hawk. I looked at them, and he continued, "Do you see how they are all the same? They are trees, and yet they are all so different." I contemplated how around me was a willow tree, an oak tree, and a eucalyptus tree—beautiful individual species of the same life form, living together harmoniously. God continued speaking to me, "The tree's existence depends on its diversity. If every single tree were exactly the same, they would all die. So it is with me, my survival depends on the *diversity* of my love. Every individual expression of the human spirit is a note and when these notes are played together, they become a symphony, a symphony of the soul, and that is my voice—the voice of God."

It was a profound experience for me—the trees

surrounding me became a metaphor for the magnificent diversity of the human spirit. Whether we express that as organized religion like Christianity, Judaism, Islam, or Buddhism, or as individuals living a spiritual life, it is all essential—every single individual instrument and note is essential for God to have a voice.

Inspired by this revelation is the following list of trees that are particularly aligned to the goal of bewitching a man. As you work with the magick of trees, allow their effects to grow and flourish in your life, giving you strength, shelter, and energy to achieve your diverse dreams.

TREE MAGICK

Doing tree magick is so simple. Choose a tree from the list below whose qualities are aligned with your needs and goals. Pour a little water on its roots, and ask for the tree's blessings before you head out on a date. If a twig or stick lies at the base of the tree, take it with you as a good-luck charm for your bewitching efforts. Leave offerings—tie a ribbon to a branch and say "thank you" to the tree for its continued good blessings. Hug a tree, kiss a tree, and wrap a strand of your hair around a tree leaf. Sit with your back

Bewitch a Man

against a tree for half an hour, and let its spiraling energy suffuse you and empower you. When you write your will, ask that one of the sacred trees be planted on your grave (as the ancient Celts did).

THE TOP THREE TREES OF BEWITCHERY
willow

The willow is a feminine tree aligned with the moon and the goddesses of young love, like Persephone. Ancient moon priestesses would gather in the willow groves to do divination and prophecy. Willow trees can heal an aching heart and bring music to the soul. The Celts would use willow wood to make their harps, which provided the music of their spiritual storytelling and the only way knowledge was passed on in their culture. (They never wrote anything down—just passed on songs of knowledge.)

THE "WILLOW TREE" SPELL

To know if a man truly loves you, pick a leaf from a willow tree. Ask the willow tree to make the truth be known to you. Throw the leaf above your head. If it spirals down, he loves you now. If it floats down, he does not love you . . . yet!

---

fig

Fig-tree energy is "food for the soul," especially when you are feeling empty and worn out. It grants the stamina to experience love in your life. The fruit of the fig is an aphrodisiac, sacred to Dionysus, the Greek god of ecstasy. Eating it can be a sensual activity, alone or with your lover.

THE "FIG TREE" SPELL

Pluck a fresh, ripe fig from a tree and kiss the tree in thanks. Sit with your back against the tree, and with your left hand on your heart and your right hand gently holding the fig, start to slowly squeeze the fig so that is splits apart in your hand. As you do this, say these words:

I open myself to joy and abundance.
I devour pleasure and passion.

Now eat the fig, licking and sucking it from your fingers in a slow, sensual way. You will have really raunchy sex within seven days! Or even straightaway (especially if you do this spell with your lover!).

---

cherry

The cherry tree is aligned with beauty and purity, and astrologically with Venus—the goddess of love.

Bewitch a Man

When cherry trees blossom, it signals the coming of spring, when new energies and new love can blossom.

THE "CHERRY TREE" SPELL

Sit under a cherry tree and let its petals fall down upon you so that you are showered in blessings of new blossoming love. Tie a pink ribbon to a branch with the initials of the man you want to fall in love with you written on it. As long as the tree blossoms, you have an opportunity to bewitch him. Even if he was previously unavailable and not interested, he will make his interest known to you very shortly afterward. When he is yours, make sure you go back to the tree and leave an offering. Pour some springwater on its roots and thank it for its help in bringing new love to your life.

MOON MAGICK

Everyone is familiar with sunbathing, but have you thought of moonbathing? The light that radiates upon the land from a full moon can empower you with powerful love-attraction energy. The moon is a symbol of the goddess Selene, the maiden of the moon who is patron goddess of love and sensuality.

To prepare yourself to moonbathe, rather than applying suntan lotion, make this moon potion.

MOON POTION

You will need the following:

- Four cups of springwater in which you have soaked one handful each of the herbs yarrow and meadowsweet (you can get these from most health food stores and supermarkets, but if you have trouble, you can substitute two handfuls of dried lavender)

(Please note: Don't boil the herbs in the water. You can warm the water to body temperature if you like, and the herbs need to soak for at least an hour.)

Strain well.

Before moonbathing take a shower, washing your hair and letting any tension or negativity swirl away down the drain.

Now pour the moon potion over your bare skin and gently pat yourself dry, leaving its residue on your bare body.

You can now choose whether to put on a moon-bathing suit (i.e., bikini) or remain sky clad. Wrap a soft blanket or towel around you, and step outside before

Bewitch a Man

releasing it to the ground and revealing your body in the moonlight. Stretch out on the ground, enjoying the delicate sensation of moonlight upon your bare skin. Enjoy your own unique and perfect beauty, and then say the following words:

Moonlight painting me with purity,
bless me and enlighten me
so that every day I radiate your glow,
and to and from me love will flow.

Lie there luxuriating in the moonlight, and then wrap your blanket back around you, go inside, and relax in bed with a gorgeous inspirational book of love stories. Do this every full moon and you will always inspire love in the hearts of men.

MOON CHART

The different phases of the moon correspond to different magickal energies for you to harness and use to your advantage when spell casting. Use the following guide to maximize all your bewitching efforts.

WAXING

(when the moon starts as a crescent shape low in the early evening sky, beginning its two-week journey to full moon)

This is a great time to conjure new love, increase passion in a current relationship, and bring all things to you that satisfy your heart's desire.

FULL

(when the moon is ripe and round in the sky)

The full moon is a great time for magick of all sorts, and you can actually work with its energy the day before, the day of, and the day after its full peak. If you make love on a full moon, watch out because you are likely to get pregnant!

WANING

(when the moon starts to fade from full to dark, becoming a crescent again)

The two weeks of the waning moon is a good time for magickal activities that affirm letting go of things that no longer serve you—like love that has gone sour, debilitating personal habits, fears, insecurities, and anything else that prevents you from experiencing happiness in love.

Bewitch a Man

DARK

(when there is no moon in the sky)

This three- to four-day period is a good time to do divination activities, whether it be tarot readings or spells to divine who is right for you—or just have a magickal rest.

HEXING ASSHOLES

TO BEWITCH THE RIGHT MAN YOU MAY HAVE TO GO through a few wrong men to get there. And as much as we Bewitchers know that we have the power to conjure what we need, we still have to bow to the fact that sometimes, despite our best efforts, our magick may misfire or we may get duped. Unfortunately, there are guys out there who are just plain old assholes, losers, or tricksters. But it's not always evident from the start. And sometimes the lessons from a difficult relationship are important to help us grow and evolve to be ready for the right guy. But there are times when enough is enough, and instead of getting sexy, it's time to get hexy!

No matter how jaded you are from failed relationships, please know there *are* good guys out there. As long as you keep your Bewitcher "BS Detector" on full alert, you can steer your way through the obstacles lacing your path to get to him, knowing the obstacles are not there to stop you. They are there to guide you to a better opportunity.

TURNING ON YOUR BEWITCHER BS DETECTOR

A Bewitcher BS Detector (BSD) can help you decide what to do in the following cases:

- You have bewitched a man, but he is misbehaving and you need help deciding what to do with him.

- You are trying to decide whether the guy you recently bewitched, who hasn't called, is worth continuing to cast spells on.

- You are in a long-term bewitched situation but are a bit bored and wondering if maybe it's *your* BS that is dragging down the relationship, or if he really is just a boring, grumpy bum.

It's really important to use your Bewitcher BS Detector anytime you feel like you are losing control. We live busy lives, and sometimes this can distract us from our best attempts as Bewitchers to bewitch a man worthy of our love and capable of returning the love we want. Sometimes despite our best intentions, we can get sucked back into the games that guys play, and before we know it, we are unempowered, crying ourselves to sleep, calling our girlfriends, and reinforcing our woes and negative self-opinion by going over and over every little confusing, mean, and depressing thing a guy has said or done to us.

As mortal women we often put up with less than great behavior from men because we are convinced we will never meet anyone better. Bewitchers do not think like that; we know that we can conjure the man of our dreams—but only by clearly recognizing what is unacceptable as far as our needs being met.

To make your Bewitcher BS Detector kit, you will need a box to keep all of the following in:

- Four identical plain heavy-cardboard cards (on one side of each, you will write "Yes," "No," "Another chance," and "Hex his ass")
- One die from a pair of dice

- Incense with scent that is strong and heady, to lull you into a meditative state (Nag Champa and Red Current by Votivo are excellent—but use any relaxing favorite.)
- Blindfold
- Little black notebook
- Black ink pen

Light the incense and take a few deep breaths, stilling your mind. Place the cards facedown and mix them so you have no idea which one is which. Next, line them in a row horizontally. In your book, write the date and the situation that has led to you using your BSD.

Decide on a question and write it down in your black book.

For example, you might ask these questions:

"Should I see this guy again?"

"Is he lying to me?"

"Am I lying to myself?"

"Is he full of BS?"

"Am I full of BS?"

"Is this the love of my bewitching life?"

Based upon the ancient divination methods and the trials and errors of thousands, it has been determined that the BS Detector is good for only four questions per session and only one session per week. So think carefully as to what your questions will be. And pay close attention to the answers.

When you are ready, open your eyes and throw the die. Whichever number comes up, count your cards, starting from the left, and count one per card. If the die landed on the number five or six, go back to the far left card after you've counted to four. When you reach the number you threw on the die, turn the card over and you have your answer. Make a note of it next to your question. Before asking the next question, shuffle the cards again, and lay them out left to right. Repeat the procedure.

When you have your four questions written and your answers provided, pick up your blindfold and slowly place it over your eyes. Inhale the sweet relaxing incense, and meditate on the questions and answers that are written before you. Know that the right course of action will be revealed to you after you say these words slowly and with great intent:

Veils of illusion part.
I remove the mask.
I know my heart.

Bewitch a Man

Slowly remove the blindfold and write down the course of action that your subconscious has revealed to you. Let the words flow. Don't second-guess them, and trust that you have the ability to divine what you need to know.

When you have finished writing, close your black book, pack everything back into your BS Detector box, and take the necessary action.

The BS Detector is based on two highly honored, ancient divination skills—tarot and numerology— and when you work with the cards and numbers in this way, you are tapping into a collective wisdom that has the answers that you need to know.

It is like a mirror that you can turn on yourself to work out where his BS ends and yours begins. Here is an example of an extremely helpful result I achieved using my BS Detector. I was two months into a relationship with a guy I liked very much and who had seemed superkeen on me but in the previous few weeks had started to pull away. After two weeks of crying myself to sleep over another perceived failed relationship, I used my BS Detector and I had the following revelation: The person who had actually made me the most unhappy in those two weeks was . . . ME! I was wallowing in self-pity and throwing away my power. I refocused and was able to let the relationship blossom again, and we got back on the right track! It eventually was revealed that he liked me a lot and had actually gotten nervous about how much he was feeling for me, and that's why he had pulled away.

Men worth bewitching take pleasure in your unique personality and appearance. If he expects you to be an airbrushed, bland, two-dimensional, half-porn-star/half-his-mother kind of girl—then he is definitely not worth bewitching. Know that if you snare a guy like this with magickal methods, he will never ever make you truly happy, or challenge you or evolve with you or inspire you. We Bewitchers need to weed out these guys and give the good guys a chance to rear their heads and blossom into our lives. So don't EVER put up with crap—use your BS Detector and hex his ass if advised, and in any case, do a self-empowerment spell and move on.

THREE STRIKES AND YOU'RE OUT

One of the first things you need to do to bewitch the right man is not decide what you want, but what you *don't* want. You need to set your parameters of pleasure and allow the bounty of the universe to flow toward you in a way that conspires in your favor.

THE "THREE STRIKES AND YOU'RE OUT" RULE

There can always be extenuating circumstances as to why a guy might break a promise or prioritize his mates, car, or mother over you. Being a Bewitcher does not mean being a bitchy diva. But it does mean drawing the line somewhere. The "Three Strikes and You're Out" rule comes into play when you give the guy three chances to show you that he is worthy of your attention. But if he fails three times, that's it—he is out. Your energy is better spent elsewhere.

THE "THREE STRIKES" RITUAL

You will need these items:

- Piece of paper
- Pen
- Half cut lemon (lemon purifies)
- Salt (salt protects)
- Black candle (black banishes)
- Envelope

Light the candle and sprinkle salt around you in a circle. Write your three-strikes list by the light of the black candle. Your list needs to be specifically tailored to your needs and experiences, stating what you don't want to experience and won't put up with in a relationship.

Once you have written your list, use the cut lemon to trace a big X over it, from corner to corner of the page. Put the list in the envelope and place under your mattress. The ritual is complete. If you are setting out to bewitch a new man, you will be less likely to encounter any of the three strikes in his behavior, and if for some reason a couple of things do sneak through, you can reread your list and know when it is time for him to go. Likewise, if you are already in a relationship, you will know when it is time to ditch him.

There are some obvious things that have a "*One* Strike and You're Out" rule:

- Lies
- Cruelty
- Violence
- Belittling
- Disrespect

A SPELL TO GET RID OF HIM

You have bewitched a guy but now decide he is just not right for you. Without wishing him harm, here's an enchanted way to get him out of your hair.

Write his name on paper and then burn it. Gather the ashes and place them in a double-sided compact mirror. Close and bind it with black ribbon, cord, or sticky tape. As you do this, recite these words:

Bewitch a Man

Our time is over, passion is spent.
It's time for you to leave my space
with haste and honor and good grace.
For the good of all, my spell is cast.
No resistance—the past is past.

Place the mirror somewhere he frequents in either his home or his office or even his car. His energy will be reflected back to himself, and he will let go of the desire to contact you. If you decide, however, that you want him back, you have to go and get the mirror and unbind it! So make sure you definitely want him out of your life, because this spell is a tricky one to reverse.

THE "I'M NOT IN LOVE" SPELL

Sometimes despite all the proof in the world that the guy is not right for you, you still can't get that "love feeling" out of your heart and mind, nor stop romanticizing the memory of him. This spell is simple and strong and will help burn away the sick knot in your stomach so you can move on to meeting the right guy.

You will need these items:

- One black candle
- One candleholder
- Sharp knife

Take the candle and turn it upside down, chipping away at the bottom with the knife to expose the wick. Carve the initials of the person you need to release from your love radar. Lick your thumb and trace over the initials with your spit, saying the following:

I release thee.

Place the candle upside down in the holder and let it burn all the way down. It will reverse your love, and you will be free of that person's stranglehold on your heart. Feel free to perform this spell a few times whenever you need it. Sometimes, for severe love-sickness, I advise that it be done at least once a week for three weeks, as twenty-one days is usually the time it takes to completely break a habit.

"Meeting Fiona was truly an act of the goddess. At the time, I was in an emotionally and verbally abusive relationship and, needless to say, felt powerless.

Through Fiona's psychic counsel and expertise in bewitchery, and with the help of the 'I'm Not in Love' spell, I felt lighter, more powerful, more feminine, free, more me, and less 'in love' with the wrong guy. I truly came to understand what real love is and how to start bewitching the right man."

—GEORGIA, JOURNALIST, LOS ANGELES

A SINCERE JUSTIFICATION FOR HEXING

The three rules of modern spell casting are as follows:

- Do what you want, but don't hurt anyone. (But what if he has already hurt you?)
- Do what you will, but don't interfere with another's free will.
  (But what if he has interfered with your free will by seducing you and then dumping you?)
- And the biggie: As you send out, so returns threefold.

Energy is all about ebb and flow. The biggest fear people have about hexing is that they are sending out bad energy and it will come back to them threefold. But what if you have already been hit with the negative threefold energy (basically, his appalling behavior and the sadness and upheaval it has caused in your life)? So consider this—that perhaps your job now is to be the flow. Let that threefold bad energy flow away from you and back to its source with a carefully chosen hex. In being returned in this way, it can end the bad-energy exchange literally by "shorting itself out."

Be aware, though, if you hex for no reason other than to be vengeful and spiteful—that law *will* apply, and a bad hex will wreak havoc in *your* life, not his.

HEX THE BASTARD

The following spells are hard-core hexes for the bastards that really deserve it. You are not going to be invoking death or injury to these guys—just making them feel some of the suffering they inflicted on you.

I know I am going to inspire the ire of some modern witches with this stance, but honestly, I am so over wishy-washy witchcraft where we turn the other cheek for the good of all, with harm to none. I have always been careful about "not breaking the witches' laws"—particularly not interfering with another's free will, and doing what we want while not hurting another—but at times I have wondered where this gets me. Guys still manage to behave appallingly. Why should we not interfere with a guy's free will and hex him if he truly deserves it?

Men have been interfering with *our* free will for years. Destruction and rebirth are nature's way, and sometimes wreaking some destruction is the necessary action to create a positive balance. Again, you are not going to harm anyone with these spells—but you will give the bastard some grief, and the universe can decide just how much he deserves and what lesson he needs to learn from it.

THE "DRIVE-BY" RITUAL

This was inspired by an experience I had where a guy came on really strong to me. We were working on a film together, so I never went there with him (I never shag on the job). But he was so charming and sincere (it seemed) for over a month, and I really felt we had become friends first, and so when the film wrapped, I succumbed to his persistent advances. We had an amazing week of incredible lovemaking and breakfasts in bed and deep heartfelt conversations. I honestly thought this guy was THE ONE. I trusted him. He had never been married and he said he was ready to be with the right girl and he gave me every impression that he thought I was going to be her. I was overjoyed.

But, after we parted at the end of that magickal week, he didn't call. And then, over a week later when he finally did, he was very casual about seeing me. We got together a few more times over a month, but he often wouldn't return my calls or he would cancel plans. He would tell me he missed me terribly when we did speak—saying he had been busy working crazy hours—and I believed him. But his hot and cold behavior was confusing and twisting me up inside. He was saying amazing, loving things to me but acting like someone who didn't care about my needs at all.

Finally I decided to drive by his house on a night when he had said he would call me and take me to a movie, since it was eleven p.m. and he still hadn't called. I drove toward his house and parked around the corner. As I snuck up the side path to his house and the open kitchen window, I could hear voices coming from inside. Through the blinds I saw him naked, holding two glasses of wine, and I could see the naked legs of a girl on the couch and I could hear her giggling.

Now, you may think that I pounded on the door, screaming bloody murder. But I didn't. I left quietly. The next day he called me and said, "Hey, baby doll, I am so sorry I didn't call you last night. I had to work late and I came home totally beat and crashed."

Bewitch a Man

"That's okay, I understand," I said. I never told him what I had seen and heard. I am too dignified. I had my answer—I wasn't crazy, the guy was lying to me. The idiot rang me a few times after that, but I was always politely busy and eventually he went away.

I had to work very hard on not hating men after this (at the time, it was the straw that broke the camel's back for me). He was so incredibly two-faced, and people who behave so appallingly, often, ultimately, bring on their own shitty karma. But, with someone like him, I figure it doesn't hurt to speed up the process a bit.

If you catch a guy behaving like this, don't directly confront him—just hex his ass with this drive-by ritual.

You will need the following:

- A dark night
- Black clothing and black cap
- Nine rusty nails (if you can't get rusty ones, bang them with a hammer and rough them up a bit)
- Dirt from a crossroad near his house (or wherever he stayed most of the time you were together)
- A car (yours or a fellow Bewitcher's who is helping you out)

Make yourself as inconspicuous as possible. It is good if he is not home when you do this. If he is home, though, the spell can actually work better because you can channel into your hex the energy inside you that just wants to bang on his door and explode with fury. But, you should not draw attention to the fact that you are there. Under NO circumstances should you confront him, because he will just write you off as a crazy, jealous bitch, and your magick will have no power over him.

Go up to the front door of his home. If he lives in an apartment building, you have to get into the building and to the door of his apartment. You need to place the nine nails and the dirt in front of his door. (Hopefully, he has a thick mat you can put them under, but if he doesn't, just pile them at the front of the door—though they may get swept away.) The spell works best if the stuff stays there, because as he repeatedly steps over the objects when he enters and leaves his house, they will continue to recharge the spell.

You are going to call on the dark goddess Hecate, who likes to dwell at crossroads and is a goddess who brings retribution and punishment as necessary—but always with a view toward bestowing harsh lessons on only those who deserve them. Hecate is a divine manifestation of the scales of balance in the universe, and you can trust her to make him suffer as he truly deserves.

Bewitch a Man

Place the nine nails side by side, and then sprinkle the dirt over them and mutter the following:

Hecate, I call on thee.
Smite [his name] for hurting me.
Punishment comes in three.
Curse him as he deserves to be.

Then get the hell out of there. He will have three weeks of really bad luck and drama. He will be stressed and unhappy, and if he is screwing around on any other girls like he did with you, they will all wise up and leave him after realizing he is a miserable bastard. Just think, you are performing a service to your sisters in making this creep accountable for his appalling behavior.

The effects will end after three weeks—so if you suffer any karmic fallout from hexing him, which is a possibility (remember the witches' law is "As you send out, so returns threefold"), it will then end for you, too. But you never know. The universe might decide to bless you with good luck since you have put an end to fellow sisters' suffering and misery at the hands of this gonzo. No matter what, any fallout, bad or good, will end in three weeks.

DREAM A LITTLE DREAM OF ME (ACTUALLY, LET'S MAKE THAT A "NIGHTMARE")

This is for the guy who said you were the only girl in his life but, you have found out, is sleeping with a bunch of hapless females and abusing all of you—physically, mentally, emotionally, and spiritually. You want nothing more to do with the loser, but before you walk out of his life, you can leave him with a lasting, magickal, torturous reminder of you.

Go to his house, pretending everything is great. When you leave, make sure you leave your underpants tucked well under his mattress. Do this with the intent to haunt him with thoughts of you. Choose a moment when he has gone to the bathroom or something, and you have privacy to do this spell properly. As you hide your undies well, say the following under your breath:

You shall have no rest.
Thoughts of me shall haunt you,
and others' love elude you.

Smile sweetly and leave him for good—never return his phone calls. He will not be able to stop thinking about you and will wonder why no girl will get into his bed. He may be able to get them close, but they will not get between the sheets—they will be repelled by your undies' hex. Hey, you are doing them a favor warding them away from this creep.

A ROADSIDE HEX

This spell works particularly well if you do not want to go anywhere physically near the guy who has hurt you. It is quick to cast, but its effects can be enormous—especially if he has projected a lot of negativity at you. This spell feeds on his darkness. The greater a bastard he is, the greater the calamity he will experience.

You will need these items:
- Photo of him
- Two sewing pins
- Black ink pen
- Piece of white paper
- Two black candles
- Patchouli incense (sacred to Hecate, goddess of retribution)
- Dirt
- Small spade (to dig a hole)

Light the candles and incense, and on the back of the photograph write his name with the black pen. On the piece of paper write a list of all the ways he has hurt you and why he deserves to be hexed. Focus hard and let your hurt and anger pour forth. Stick the two pins into his photograph so that they form an X over his face. Spit on the photograph, and then fold the white paper over it. Bury this at least four inches into the ground. One of the best places to do this is at a crossroad. Hecate dwells at crossroads, as she is a goddess who brings balance and retribution. As you dig your hole, ask for her blessings and help in bringing justice to your horrible guy.

Bewitch a Man

Place the paper and photo inside the hole and cover with dirt. Stamp on the soil hard with your foot three times and walk away without looking back.

OOPS, I HAVE CHANGED MY MIND

You want to *reverse* a hex. Perhaps you have decided that you would rather take the high road and heal yourself and move on rather than continue to stay bound to this person, albeit through a hexing spell rather than a personal relationship. (Remember, as long as your hexing spell stays in effect, you are energetically and karmically connected to the person.) Or, Goddess forbid, you hexed the wrong person (in which case your hex won't work well because hexes only work effectively on those who deserve to receive them from you).

Reversing a hex is possible. It usually requires a physical deconstruction of the spell.

By the light of seven white candles, write a description of your hex on paper. Burn it and sprinkle some salt into the ashes as you say these words:

I purify my hex.
The magick is gone.

The anger is spent.
Where once there was hate
love and light now illuminate.

Dispose of the salted ashes either by mixing them into the earth or throwing them into the trash. Any negativity in the hexed person's life caused by your spell will rapidly dissipate. And you will move forward in love and light.

GOOD LIVING IS STILL THE BEST REVENGE

Yes, I have provided hexes here. But I want to emphasize that at least 90 percent (well, let's make that a more realistic 80 percent) of the time, you will get more satisfaction from healing yourself and moving on from an awful situation with a guy than from staying connected to him by hexing him and perpetuating all the awful negative energy. The best revenge is for him to see you out looking superhappy with some superhot guy—or even better, to hear through your mutual friends that you have moved on and are happy and thriving without him.

Bewitch a Man

Chapter Twelve

GODDESSES ARE PEOPLE TOO

YOU DON'T NEED TO LOOK SO FAR TO FIND YOUR inspiration. Goddesses are all around you if you only open your eyes and your heart.

Bewitchers know that the more often they can join with other like-minded magickal sisters and experience potent bewitching moments together, the more wonderful life becomes and the more love there is to be experienced. When Bewitchers fuel and encourage each other, they become more than the sum of their parts, and the positive energy generated becomes a powerful magnet that will consistently attract better men and better love experiences in each of the Bewitchers' lives.

"Fiona created an extraordinary love spell for me and my girlfriends, which we cast at my 'pre-Valentine, all-girl, lingerie party.' There we were, fourteen girls in lingerie, dancing on a bed of rose petals in a circle of candlelight, chanting our love spell. It was a most enlightening and exhilarating experience, which each of us are still talking about! And the next day we all had a beautiful and love-filled Valentine's Day!"
—FELICIA, INTERIOR DESIGNER, LOS ANGELES

LOVE MAGICK PARTY

This is the ultimate love spell, where Bewitchers can join together to magnify love in their lives. The motto of this spell is "Too much love is not enough!" When Bewitchers gather together in comradeship and with combined intent, the magick works very fast and very powerfully. As a part of this bash, you will need to designate the "high flower priestess," one who will lead the ritual and make the enchanted candied rose petals. They cannot just be bought at a store. The Bewitcher making them will be conjuring magick into them—it's a major part of the spell.

Send an invite to your fellow Bewitchers, saying that you are having a Love Magick Party, telling them there will be feasting followed by a fun group spell casting. Clothing should be all white and goddesslike, or if you want to make the magick work not only in your love lives but your sex lives too, you can all wear glamorous lingerie! Serve a light, luscious supper and lovely French champagne and other suitably indulgent refreshments and sweet treats.

RAPTUROUS ROSE PETALS

Procure enough rose petals from your florist or, better yet, your garden, so that everyone gathered can have one each, minimum. Make sure the flowers have not been sprayed with insecticide or any other chemicals. Rinse the petals gently in cool water and place on white paper towels. Gently blot them dry and leave for half an hour to air-dry. In a small bowl, mix two teaspoons powdered egg whites and two teaspoons warm water. Stir gently with a wire whisk for two minutes to allow the powder to absorb into the water. Then beat briskly until the powder is completely dissolved and foamy.

Using a small, clean, new artist paintbrush, lightly cover petals with a thin, even coat of egg-white mixture. Coat each side of each petal.

Now, to make magickal, repeat this incantation for each petal as you coat it:

Love so sweet and strong,
so pure and delicate,
more than can be imagined,
blessed and heaven sent

While the petals are still moist, sprinkle them lightly with extra-fine sugar. Shake off excess sugar. Allow the "rapturous" petals to dry completely, uncovered, on waxed paper for at least four hours or overnight. You can store the petals in a tightly covered container between layers of waxed paper for up to eleven days in a cool, dark cupboard. (But not in the fridge—you don't want your love to go cold!)

Create the flower chamber, concocting an environment that is divinely beautiful and delicately empowered.

The flower chamber features these things:
- Big circle of white, scented candles
- Lots of soft, sweetly scented rose petals scattered on the floor
- Your "rapturous rose petals" arranged on a pretty plate
- Fabulous music that gives you goose bumps and makes you want to dance

Bewitch a Man

The ritual is simple—everyone dances to one tune, declared the bewitching song, barefoot like princesses on the rose petals, doused in blessed candlelight illuminating everyone's inner and outer beauty.

As you dance, you are raising energy—in traditional magick it is called "raising the cone of power"—so dance with intent. The intent of not so much *seeing* your beauty as *feeling* it, and knowing it radiates and blesses all men that it shines upon.

Dance with abandon, dance in celebration. If you are single while you dance, it is the time to conjure the vision of the man you want to bewitch in your mind. If you are in a "budding" relationship or a long-term one that you are empowering, see your man in your mind's eye and dance with him. Join with your fellow goddesses and dance for love!

When you are flushed and happy and bursting with love and appreciation for yourself and one another, marveling at how special you all are and how awesome it is that you together take time out from your everyday lives to create this beautiful, meaningful, adventurous moment, each person picks up a rapturous rose petal and lets it melt on her tongue.

The high flower priestess says this magickal incantation, which everyone repeats before placing the rapturous rose petal on their tongue.

Love so sweet and strong,
pure and delicate,
more than can be imagined,
blessed and heaven sent

Know as you do this that the magick that was invoked as the rapturous petals were made is now infusing you with enchanted love and potent magnetism, right through to the core of your being. You are Bewitchers, blessed with an abundance of romance and joy that will continue to blossom and grow in the coming days.

THE "YOUR SISTERS ARE NOT YOUR RIVALS" RITUAL

How blessed we are to have amazing role models around us, the women in our families and at our jobs, our dear friends, and even a stranger standing next to us on the subway. For every broken-heart story we hear, there is a happy-heart story. Love is as perennial

Bewitch a Man

as the grass (as the gorgeous saying goes), and there really is enough to go around. Celebrate the excellence in your fellow females—and in doing so, you will empower yourself.

Try this exercise (it's not a spell, but you can use the list you create in one later).

PART ONE

Get a piece of paper, and going back in your memory as far as you can, write down the name of every female that comes into your head whom you have had some kind of personal relationship with. It can be good (your beloved sister) or bad (perhaps the girl who "stole" your ex-boyfriend—even though she did you a favor, as you can see now he was a jerk).

PART TWO

Next to their names, write something about them worthy of your respect and adoration that you have personally witnessed. This may be easy when it comes to your favorite sister but a lot harder when thinking of someone who wronged you.

The first person that jumped into my head was an old school friend Michelle who wronged me by just deciding one day to ignore me. It was decreed by the cool group at school that I wasn't worthy of their companionship, and Michelle decided to follow the flock. At the time it was terribly distressing to me. She and I had been joined at the hip for two years, and now I was just cast away. It was really hard to think of something good in her. But once I moved past the hurt feeling, I remembered that she had had a crazy, fun, good-natured sense of humor and used to always crack me up (when she was speaking to me!). In seeing the innate goodness in her ability to make people laugh, I was also able to recognize that her poor behavior resulted from her own insecurities. She was attempting to fit in at school as much as I was, and unfortunately, I had to carry the brunt of her efforts.

As you create your list of females, know this: Everything good that you recognize in them is a quality and ability that resonates in you. It really does take one to know one.

PART THREE

Know that the more you are inspired and excited by (and in some cases, forgiving of) the females you cross paths with in life, the more you will see them as fellow inhabitants you can take or leave rather than as rivals you need to be threatened by.

Bewitch a Man

And this is one of the most important qualities in a Bewitcher: knowing that our sisters are not our rivals and there are enough men to go around—and that if the hideous girls get the guys, that just means the guys are hideous too, and they are not even worth bewitching!

BEWITCHERS TAKE MANY FORMS AND ARE AS VARIED AND AMAZING AS THE WOMEN THAT LIVE ON THIS PLANET

If you enjoyed the "Not Your Rivals" ritual, you may like to expand on it and write an essay on one or more women who have totally inspired you. I decided to do this as I was writing this book, and I would like to share my essay with you.

MY TWO MOTHERS— BEWITCHERS EXTRAORDINAIRE

I am adopted, and in the last few years I have had the interesting experience of having two mothers. Meeting my biological mother was initially very confrontational but ultimately has become very (and increasingly) rewarding. My early relationship with my mother who raised me was also very confrontational (for different reasons, though!) but has now evolved to be very rewarding. I can see how these two women have been huge influences on my life and who I am, in very different and yet compatible ways.

MY MOTHER ERIKA

My biological mother and I had a long New Year's Eve chat on the phone during the time I was writing this book. She exclaimed to me, "At the age of sixty-three I am having the time of my life!" She is a beauty therapist, and her privately owned beauty salon, manned exclusively by her, is booked two years in advance, and her "ladies" (clients) are like family. She is so happy with her life—sixty-three and single. Completely single and happy to stay that way for the rest of her life.

Did she bewitch men in her life? Yes, there were a few. Her first husband was so bewitched by her, he went nuts, and was so jealous of her beauty that he beat her and kidnapped her to Turkey. He locked her up in his bedroom so that no other man could lay eyes on her—but she escaped with the help of his wily and sympathetic mother, who took pity on the poor little German girl with the broken nose who cowered in the corner of her son's bedroom every morning when she took in his cup of Turkish tea.

Bewitch a Man

And then there was my father, who, although he could not marry her, employed her for twenty-four years at his company.

And then there was her second and last husband, who stole all her money and put her in a road accident that saw her foot torn off and her back broken, and she was pronounced medically deceased on the operating table. But she then revived. The surgeons reattached her foot, and she used therapy and positive visualization to heal her broken back. (Doctors at the time considered her a bit of a medical miracle with the success of her recovery and rehabilitation; she says it was the power of her mind to overcome adversity.)

My mother is a Bewitcher because she rose like the noble warrioress that she is, and using positive visualization, did the impossible (according to the doctors attending her) and mended her broken back, came out of bankruptcy, and at an age when most people retire, started her own beauty business.

She is a beautiful woman who looks at least twenty years younger than her age, and men adore her and she basks in their adoration—but she chooses to be alone.

We laughed together on the phone that night, and I said, "You are sixty-three and I am about to turn forty, and we are both like two girls just stepping out into the world, with huge smiles on our faces and love and enthusiasm for life in our hearts!"

I am privileged to have a biological mother like Erika, whose blood and genes pulse in my veins—she inspires me and motivates me. I have known her only a few years, and yet I have known her since I was born—her spirit in me has subtly influenced the choices I have made to live a spiritual life, to be a free-thinker, and to grow better, not older.

MY MOTHER BARBARA

My mother Barbara is a Bewitcher because she has been married to my father for over forty years. They have raised three kids and have grandchildren now. You may think it was the era they married in that ensures their attachment—but if I really look at my mother, I can see she is a Bewitcher. While creating a home environment for my father and family, she has maintained her own work. She makes my dad laugh. She doesn't let him rattle her. She was a traditional wife in that she did the housework and ran the house when Dad went off to his full-time job—but now that they are both retired, he helps out too.

My mother is an inspirational Bewitcher because

Bewitch a Man

she is in her power—she embraces her choices and excels at them. And she has kept her man by her side through thick and thin for longer than I have been alive. Although we are very different people who have made very different choices in our lives, she inspires me greatly.

ROSALEEN NORTON

To close I would like to introduce you to a favorite heroine of mine who I think embodies the essence that beats in the hearts of true Bewitchers. Rosaleen Norton was a bohemian artist who lived in the notorious Kings Cross district of Sydney, Australia, in the fifties and sixties. Born during a violent thunderstorm, her life mirrored that entrance. She said she was a witch, and with her exotic appearance, alternative spirituality, and remarkably provocative and popular esoteric artwork, there was no doubt that she was. She is the ultimate personal Bewitcher icon of mine. So much so that when I shot Australian *Playboy* (before being featured in USA *Playboy*), I celebrated her by re-creating scenes from her life. One of my favorite shots is of me drinking coffee, naked, in a smoky dark coffeehouse in Kings Cross. It was inspired by the stories that Rosaleen would go to this very café and model nude for the art students in a small studio upstairs. Then she would walk down the spiral staircase at the back of the store to order a coffee and sit in the front bay window to enjoy it—still naked.

Behavior like that now would still draw a lot of attention—but Rosaleen was doing this in the 1950s! She was truly beholden to no one's opinion. Bold and free, she took lovers as it pleased her, courting an eclectic selection of men, who included a poet, a famous conductor, and a young artist. Her final partner before her death in 1979 was a man twenty years her junior.

She worshipped the pagan male god of sexuality and abundance, Pan, and embodied aspects of empowerment that society attributed to being more appropriate for a man than a woman. As her notoriety grew, she was vilified, feared, and even imprisoned at one point for her freely expounded pagan attitudes. She courted drama and excitement in her life.

Rosaleen was a brilliant artist, and her work featured wild and expansive esoteric themes. At the time, her art showings were closed by police and some of her work was even destroyed because it was considered so

Bewitch a Man

subversive—a woman painting images of nude women cavorting with panthers and serpents in bacchanalian abandon (though similar work painted at the time by the artist Norman Lindsay was considered great art)! After a colorful, extraordinary, and much persecuted life, like so many brilliant artists who were ahead of their time, Rosaleen died poor and in a hospice in the late seventies. What remains of her artwork is highly valued and considered exceptional.

Her last words before she died were, "I have no regrets. I came into the world bravely, I will go out bravely."

Rosaleen teaches us that as true Bewitchers, we are beholden to no man or to the need for a man or to the opinions of men. We *choose* our company and indeed the need for company. We pursue our passions without fear of recrimination. We cast more than a few spells every week to create magick in our lives, as we choose and desire.

And inspired by Rosaleen's last words, we Bewitchers are brave and free.